The Power of

ONE DAY'S TIME

Cathy,
Its such a blessing to see you
again at St Louis camp. Your
love, and passion, for Jesus is
very evident. I pray this book
greatly encourages you, and inspires
great hope in your heart,
God Bless You Richly
In Christ
Pastor Chris Slosser
CCJSLOSSER@gmail.com

CHRIS SLOSSER

ISBN 978-1-64515-681-9 (paperback)
ISBN 978-1-64515-682-6 (digital)

Christian Faith Publishing, Inc.
832 Park Avenue
Meadville, PA 16335
www.christianfaithpublishing.com

Printed in the United States of America

Acknowledgments

I want to thank my wife, Cindy, and my dear son, Joshua, for your love, encouragement, and belief in me. You are my exceeding pride and joy.

I want to thank my parents, Carl and Nancy Slosser (my dad said to me last spring, "You need to write a book," so I followed his orders). I want to also thank my in-laws, Gerry and Chris Sattelberg, for your encouragement and affirmation of our ministry (it means a lot). Thank you to all of our family. You are all a blessing, and we are blessed by all of you.

Thank you to our church family, the Beaverton Church of God (some of the best people on planet earth, bar none), and my former church, Millington Church of God (you are amazing people). Thank you to my friend, prayer partner, confidant, and pastor (in many ways), Bill Guigear. Thank you to Glenn and Joy Knochel for your encouragement and critiques, to my friend Sonia Cano (thanks for praying for me so faithfully through the writing of this book). Enormous thanks to Jean Plude who helped in countless ways (I can't thank you enough). Thank you to all my friends, fellow believers in Christ who have believed in me, encouraged me, and prayed for me (I am a product of being surrounded by the greatest people on planet earth).

Thank you, most of all, to Jesus for being my Savior, Lord, my everything, and the priceless treasure you are.

Chris Slosser

PROLOGUE

For in this hope we were saved, but hope that
is seen is no hope at all. Who hopes for what
he already has? But, if we hope for what we
do not yet have, we wait for it patiently.
—Romans 8:24–25

To them God has chosen to make known among
the Gentiles the glorious riches of this mystery,
which is Christ in you, the hope of glory.
—Colossians 1:27

We live in a seriously messed-up world. I am talking messed up on-steroids kind of messed up; not just a mess but, as they say, a hot mess. How sad to think that a world that was created by a perfect God, in a perfect way, with the first man and first woman created perfectly and living in a perfect place, the Garden of Eden, could decline to the point which we are at today.

It is scary and very depressing to even click on the news in a day and age where there is so much dysfunction and evil running rampant. We live in a day when things that we thought were unthinkable are happening on a daily basis. Places that were once safe havens such as schools, colleges, and churches are being shot up to the heartbreak of communities and a heartbroken nation that wonders, *Where did things go so fundamentally wrong?* and *When is this ever going to end?* These are challenging and very perilous times we are living in, are they not?

On top of all this, there is rampant division between people groups. There are the liberals versus the conservatives, one race against another race, family members opposing other family members, the rich versus the poor (class warfare fueled by politicians who are supposed to be uniting, not dividing, us), and discord of all manner. We have many, many challenges facing us, as individuals and corporately, in this present world we are living in.

As a result of all this dysfunction in the home, in society, in the workplace, on social media, in the classroom, and globally as well, many people are depressed, in despair, broken, and frustrated. Many are feeling hopeless, not knowing where to turn to find peace and serenity in a world that seems, many times, to be spinning out of control.

Where can we find hope?

Where can we find peace?

Where can we find refuge?

If anywhere, at all.

If you can relate to anything I have mentioned or have asked any of the above questions, I have some very good news for you. There is a place of sure hope; there is a place of peace and rest of soul; there is a refuge from the storms of life that are raging furiously in our world today. There is hope in the Lord, in God, in Jesus who is our eternal (and sure) hope, who is the Prince of Peace, who is our sure refuge in the raging storms of life. The good news is, this God of infinite, amazing, and unfathomable grace is looking for you today! How do I know this? Because Jesus says so in his Holy Word. Jesus says in Luke 19:10, "For the Son of Man came to seek and to save what was lost."

This promise includes all of us, all who are confused, all who are broken by life, all who have lost their way or don't even know there is a way, all who are depressed, all who are oppressed, all who think, *I am not a religious person*, all who think, *I am too far gone*, all who need a second, third, or a fiftieth new start in life, all who are empty within, and all who wonder, *Why do I even exist?* If you fall into any of the above categories or any other as well, the God of sure hope, the God of salvation, the God of a brand-new beginning, in his infinite grace, is looking for you. The very reason you are reading these words is because God is wanting to speak into your life through these words.

If you are weary, tired, worn out from trying it your own way and getting nowhere or next to nowhere, if you are feeling empty and know something or someone is missing, then I feel God wants to speak strongly into your life through what I am about to share.

This is a book about hope and a hope that is sure. What do you mean by that, Chris? What I mean is that there are many things we can hope for that are not necessarily sure. For example:

"I hope I win the lotto or the Publishers Clearing House."

"I hope Ms. America or Mr. Universe comes up to me and asks me out or to marry them (let's skip the formalities, lol)." (This only applies to single people; if you are married, please disregard this illustration.)

"I hope I go to work tomorrow and have my company double my wages without any additional work responsibilities."

"I hope I get all As without having to study, apply myself, or listen to my teacher."

"I hope I have a great uncle, aunt, or long-lost relative who leaves me ten million dollars in their will."

"I hope for this, that, or the other. I hope all this, and more, comes true in my life. I hope my ship finally comes in any day now."

The truth, and I hate to say it, is that many things we hope for rarely, if ever, materialize.

However, the hope of God, of Jesus, is a sure hope because it is backed by the most reliable source there is, the one who is holy and absolutely, positively, cannot lie nor can he fail any who truly put their hope and faith in him. The hope of the Lord is a sure 1,000-percent, take-it-to-the-bank, push-all-your-chips-into-the-middle, absolute, sure hope from the God of absolute truth and who is absolutely holy. I repeat, he cannot lie nor can he fail.

In this book, we will look at many characters from the Bible who were in a very dark place, in despair, feeling empty and lost, those who were feeling hopeless, feeling that they were destined for a wretched lot in life, and those who had their whole destinies, in this life and in the next, radically changed *in one day's time* as God came on the scene and changed everything—forever.

Friends, it is my prayer that, as you read through these pages, the Holy Spirit will take these words you are about to read and speak sure hope, speak sure life, speak sure encouragement, speak sure vitality, speak sure joy, speak the sure abundance of heaven into your heart, soul, and mind. I pray that they would get so deeply embedded that you will be able to rise above any despair you may be experiencing, for God has something so much better for you, my friend.

May the love of the Lord, the hope of the Christian Gospel, the encouragement, and the enthusiasm of the Holy Spirit breathe eternal life and eternal hope into your heart. May you have a life-changing encounter with the Lord as we journey together through this book. God bless you, God strengthen you, may God encourage you, may God inspire your heart, and may God keep you as you place your hope in him. In Jesus's name, Amen!

With love in the Lord,
Pastor Chris Slosser

1

"RISE, TAKE UP YOUR BED, AND WALK"

I have heard it said, "If you preach hope, you will never lack an audience, for we live in a world longing and searching for a sure hope."

This book is about hope, about how the God of the universe, through his Son, Jesus Christ, can turn our circumstances, or supposed "lot in life," around and change everything today and for all eternity. If you yourself are in a dark place, a burdensome place, feeling like you are trapped by your circumstance, your impediments, and feeling of hopelessness, it is my prayer that the following pages will breathe hope, encouragement, and belief into your life again. There is a God who is powerful, who can come on the scene in our lives and turn our circumstances and the way we view our circumstances around radically.

In the following chapters, we will be exploring the lives of many individuals who were in a very dark place, dealing with problems far bigger than themselves and that they did not ask for (can anyone relate to that?). All these individuals were going through their days thinking it was probably going to be just another day in their wretched lives. Then Jesus came onto the scene, and everything changed for the rest of their lives and all eternity as well.

The first Bible character we are going to meet is a man who had a thirty-eight-year infirmity. He was a poor paralytic who was seeking a healing, a deliverance, that always seemed to elude him, but that was all about to change.

His story is found in John 5:1–16 in the New King James Version which reads:

> After this there was a feast of the Jews, and Jesus went up to Jerusalem.
>
> Now there is in Jerusalem by the Sheep Gate a pool, which is called in Hebrew, Bethesda having five porches.
>
> In these lay a great multitude of sick people, blind, lame, paralyzed, waiting for the moving of the water.
>
> For an angel went down at a certain time into the pool and stirred up the water; then, whoever stepped in first, after the stirring of the water, was made well of whatever disease he had.
>
> Now a certain man was there who had an infirmity 38 years.
>
> When Jesus saw him lying there and knew that he already had been in that condition a long time. He said to him, "Do you want to be made well?"
>
> The sick man answered, "Sir, I have no man to put me into the pool when the water is stirred up; but, while I am coming, another steps down before me."
>
> Jesus said to him, "Rise, take up your bed, and walk."
>
> And immediately the man was made well, took up his bed and walked. And that day was the Sabbath.
>
> The Jews, therefore, said to him who was cured, "It is the Sabbath; it is not lawful for you to carry your bed."

He answered them, "He who made me well said to me, 'Take up your bed and walk.'"

But the one who was healed did not know who it was, for Jesus had withdrawn, a multitude being in that place.

Afterwards, Jesus found him in the temple and said to him, "See, you have been made well. Sin no more, lest a worse thing come upon you."

The man departed and told the Jews that it was Jesus who made him well.

For this reason, the Jews persecuted Jesus and sought to kill Him because He had done these things on the Sabbath.

I want to challenge us, as we consider this man's story, to put ourselves in this man's sandals, the sandals in which he had never been able to walk, ever, in his whole life.

This is a man who had been an invalid (lame and paralyzed) for all of his thirty-eight years of life. This infirmity was all he had ever known. He had never walked, never knew what it was like to even try to walk, and he had to totally rely on others to get to wherever he went. Imagine the frustration he must have felt.

In addition, this man came to the pool of Bethesda, seeking healing from God, for from time to time, the angel of the Lord roiled up the waters of the pool, and the first one in would be healed (John 5:4). This healing would be on a first-come-first-served basis, and he could never beat the rest into the healing waters, though he tried frequently. This man, who desired God's healing desperately, had seen countless others receive the healing he so desperately wanted for himself. Imagine how this man must have felt.

This man was living with this terrible lifelong affliction that he never asked for or did anything to deserve. He was just born this way. This man had to deal with the constant discouragement of losing out to someone else for the thing (the healing) he so desperately wanted for himself, seeing others receive the blessing time after time.

I imagine he felt totally hopeless, frustrated, defeated, and in utter despair. I imagine he thought, *This is my lot in life, to live this wretched existence as a poor paralytic.* Imagine how it must have felt to be this man (handicapped, poor, looked down on by society, anticipating a healing touch from heaven that always seemed to come to someone else and not him). What a wretched way to live, and I am sure he thought this was going to be the way his whole life would be; "How sad, how depressing, how empty, how pathetic my life is." Maybe some, or many, of us can relate!

So this man goes down to the Bethesda pool, as he had done numerous other times, waiting to lose out to someone else on this given day. *Who am I going to lose out to today?* he must have thought. Little did he know, on this particular day, everything was about to change forever.

On this particular day, Jesus had come into town and was seeking this man out. Jesus, who had arrived in Jerusalem, did not come to admire the beauty and majesty of the temple and the holy city. He came to the pool. He came to the place where the sick people, the blind, the lame, and paralyzed, were. The God of all grace and mercy was seeking out, personally, those who needed his healing touch!

On this particular day, this infirmed man was approached by a man he did not know who asked a very peculiar question, "Do you want to be made well?" What kind of question was this? And who was it who asked such a thing?

Before he could even fully answer, the man said to him, "Rise, take up your bed, and walk."

Immediately at the sound of this stranger's voice, "My legs, my feet, which were weak and impotent, felt strong, felt alive for the very first time. Could it be that the healing I have waited my whole life for has finally come? Could this be the day I have waited all my days for? My day of healing and liberation! Is this just a dream? Have my dreams, after all this time, finally come true? I'm going to try it, to do the one thing I have seen so many others do, young and old, and that is to walk. Here goes nothing," he said to himself. Up he went, and he stayed up. For the first time in his thirty-eight years of life, he took the first steps of a lifetime more and he would take for the rest of his days—doing the one thing he had seen infants do for the very first time to the applause of cheering parents and longing that he, himself, would get to experience in his life as well. His day had finally come, brought to him by a stranger who he would later find out was the Savior of the world, Jesus Christ.

In one day's time, with one encounter with the Son of the Living God, this man's lifetime of despair, affliction, and handicap was put behind him for the rest of his lifetime. I can only imagine the joy, the ecstasy, the relief this man felt on that day and every day afterward once this day of liberation came to his life. His thirty-eight-year impediment was gone, totally and permanently, by the hand of a merciful Savior.

As we consider this beautiful story of liberation, I want to take this story from this man's arena into our arena. What does this story have for us in this day and age? For all of Scripture was recorded to speak to, not only the lives of those in Bible days but to us in this age as well.

Maybe you are reading this, and you yourself have been dealing with a long-term affliction as well, and you need a divine deliverance. It may be a physical ailment, a stronghold (a wrong pattern of thinking that continues to constantly drag you back down), an ongoing affliction that you cannot shake free from, or a whole host of other things. I have good news for you! That is this same Jesus, the liberator of this man is still in the liberating business today as well. The God of liberation then is the God of liberation now.

Hebrews 13:8 says, "Jesus Christ is the same yesterday and today and forever."

The God of liberation, the God of deliverance, the God of all heaven and earth is looking for you today. In one day's time, Jesus Christ, like we see here, can change it all as we look to him, as we look to him in faith believing. This passage tells us, "The Lord of heaven and earth seeks out the hurting, the destitute, and those who need His healing touch."

Jesus, as he entered Jerusalem, did not go to where all the "beautiful people (in their eyes, anyway)" or to where all the "whole" people were or to where the people who had it all together were (is there even such a person?). Jesus instead went to where the hurting, the afflicted, and the down and out were. That was true then, and it is true now. Jesus is never far from the afflicted, the broken, and brokenhearted.

- Jesus is there, wherever tears are shed.
- Jesus is there, wherever frustration takes place.
- Jesus is there, wherever humans are shedding tears of regret over poor choices they
- have made that hurt others badly.
- Jesus is there, wherever there is godly sorrow over sinful choices we have made.

The God of infinite mercy is close by. He longs to forgive, to heal, and to make all things new.

Psalm 51:17 says, "The sacrifices of God are a broken spirit, a broken and contrite heart, O God, you will not despise."

Where there is true brokenness, true contrition, God is nearby. He is nearby not to condemn, to spew out wrath and bring judgment but to forgive, to save, to restore, and to reform. "A broken and contrite heart, O God, you will not despise."

Jesus says these words to the broken, the weary, and the burdened in Matthew 11:28–30:

> Come to me all who are weary and burdened, and I will give you your rest. Take My yoke upon you and learn from Me, for I am gentle and humble in heart, and you will find rest for your souls, for My yoke is easy and My burden is light.

I don't know about you, but that does not sound like a divine being ready at a moment's notice to strike us dead with judgment and wrath. Rather he invites us into his mercy, his forgiveness, his rest. Do you, my friend, know this Savior of divine rest and mercy today? If not, Jesus Christ is seeking you out just like the paralytic in our Bible text. He is seeking to give you the ultimate rest, the rest of soul (Matthew 11:29). If you will open your heart to him, you will find a mercy, a rest of soul, that is perfect and divine that brings the ultimate healing within.

I conclude this chapter with a famous nursery rhyme about an egg I came to know all too well in grade school. This nursery rhyme about a famous egg went like this:

> Humpty Dumpty sat on a wall,
> Humpty Dumpty had a great fall.
> All the king's horses and all the king's men
> Could not put Humpty Dumpty back
> together again.

This nursery rhyme is not just about Humpty Dumpty. It is the human story as well.

In the beginning, God made Adam and Eve, the first human beings whom we all descend from. Adam and Eve were made perfect, in the perfect image of God (Genesis 1:26–27). Adam and Eve, however, were deceived by Satan, the enemy of our souls (Genesis 3); they, and all humanity afterward, became fallen creations, infected with a sinful nature.

Romans 5:12 says of this, "Therefore, just as sin entered the world through one man, and death through sin; and, in this way, death came to all men because all sinned."

As a result of this fall in Eden's garden, we are all like Humpty Dumpty, broken by the fall. That would be very sad and depressing if that was the end of the story. Thank God it is not. The rest of the story is this—God, in his great love and mercy, sent Jesus, his Son, on a divine rescue mission to save us, to restore us, and to put us back together again.

Jesus was sent by God to reverse the curse that all mankind fell under, committed in the Garden of Eden. Through the saving work of Jesus, done on the cross, we can be healed within, reconciled back to God, and given the gift of eternal life.

Romans 5:16–21 says of this:

> But the gift is not like the trespass. For, if the many died by the trespass of one man, how much more did God's grace and the gift that came by the grace of the One Man, Jesus Christ, overflow to the many! Again, the gift of God is not like the result of the one man's sin. The judgment followed one sin and brought condemnation, but the gift followed many trespasses and brought justification.
>
> For if, by the trespass of one man, death reigned through that one man, how much more will those who receive God's abundant provision of grace and the gift of righteousness reign in life through the One Man, Jesus Christ.
>
> Consequently, just as the result of one trespass was condemnation for all men, so also the result of one act of righteousness was justification that brings life for all men.
>
> For, just as through the disobedience of the one man, the many were made sinners, so also through the obedience of the One Man, the many will be made righteous.
>
> The law was added so that the trespass might increase, but where sin increased, grace increased all the more; so that, just as sin reigned in death, so also grace might reign through righteousness to bring eternal life through Jesus Christ our Lord.

What these above verses tell us is very great news for all humanity, great news we all need to understand and personally embrace. That great news is this—though humanity, like Humpty Dumpty, fell and was severely broken by the fall, it does not, unlike Humpty's fall, have to be a fatality. God, through his Son, Jesus, has come to save us, to gather all the pieces of our broken lives up and put us back together again as good as new.

No human efforts (i.e., all the king's horses and all the king's men) can put us back together again but praise God, Jesus can as we embrace him with faith and repentance.

Friends, there is a God who loves you (whether you believe it or know it or not). He has come through his Son, Jesus Christ, to save you, to put your broken life back together again, and to give you a brand-new lease on life. Please do not deny him by unbelief or by running away from his wide-open arms for you, the opportunity to make a miracle out of your life.

This God of great grace who said in Luke 19:10, "For the Son of Man came to seek and to save what was lost." He is looking for you today.

The question from the Lord to you is the same question he asked the paralytic, and that is simply this, "Do you want to be made well?"

The work that can bring your healing and mine was done on the cross by the Lord. Now the ball is in our court to simply embrace, believe, and receive him into our hearts, to be healed within.

CHAPTER

2

"YOUR FAITH HAS HEALED YOU"

"Go," Jesus said, "Your faith has healed
you." Immediately, he received his sight
and followed Jesus along the road.
—Mark 10:52

We live in a very fast-paced, pedal-to-the-metal, rush-rush-rush
world where we have places to be, people to see, and a large laundry
list of things to get done—continually. Life in 2018 is a life-in-the-
fast-lane kind of world especially in America where I live.

As I was considering the fast-paced nature of our world, I
thought about the story of the good Samaritan. The thing that really
struck me about this story was how the two religious figures were so
agenda-driven that they passed right on by the wounded traveler, the
one they—of all people—were called to help and come to the aid
of. The despised Samaritan, however, and not those who professed
religion, was the one who took the time, gave of his resources, and
nursed this wounded traveler back to wholeness. Once again, Jesus,
when he told this story, said for us as believers to learn from the
example of this good Samaritan and "Go and do likewise" (Luke
10:25–37).

As I read this passage, I became very convicted myself. How
many times have I been the priest or the Levite in this story and

not the good Samaritan? How many times have I, in pursuing my personal agenda, walked right on by wounded, hurting people and not stopped to help like I should? It's very easy to do especially in the fast-paced, agenda-driven world like the one we live in. I am a pastor, a person of the cloth, and I know that I have failed, from time to time, to be the good Samaritan that I have been called to be. And if we are honest, my fellow believers (if you are one at this point), I bet I would not be the only one guilty of passing on by when I certainly should have taken the time and given of myself to help my fellow man who has been wounded by life. We live in a world full of wounded travelers, some physically, but more who are relationally, emotionally, psychologically, and spiritually wounded who our compassion and love could potentially set back on the road to healing and wholeness.

I know I need, and am challenged by, God to be more sensitive, more on the lookout, to be more intentional about identifying and helping the walking, talking wounded who God brings along my path. I believe that I am probably not the only one who needs to step up my game in this area. I would challenge you—if you are one of those who is wounded—to let someone know, for we do live in a world that has many good Samaritans yet if they know there is a genuine need. Don't keep your pain bottled up because you don't want to inconvenience anyone. There are still a lot of grace-filled, compassionate people who will help if they know the need is there.

Our world is a very painful, evil world where there are many wounded travelers, so may we be sensitive to our fellow man and be those good Samaritans. By so doing and so being, it brings a good feeling within, and it wins the smile of Jesus who said, "Go and do likewise."

Jesus Christ was (and is) the ultimate good Samaritan. His agenda was not the agenda (the laundry list of things to do). His number 1 agenda was, and is, people. For us as his followers, people should be our number 1 agenda as well. I think we need to be reminded of that—at least, I know I do.

Jesus was about the people.

Why did Jesus die on the cross?

"For God so loved the world, he gave His only begotten Son" (John 3:16).

Why? For the people of the world.

Jesus gave us, as believers, his great commission (Matthew 28:18–20).

Why? To reach the people of this world with his Gospel.

Who is Jesus coming for at the end of the age?

With the Lord, it's always all about people. It's all about his people and the redemption and restoration of lost people, outside of Christ, getting the people of the world ready to meet their God when he comes again. In life, the main thing is to keep the main thing the main thing, not majoring on minors and minoring on majors. In Christ, the main thing is the redemption and compassionate care of people.

With that, we are going to take a look at another wounded traveler named Bartimaeus who Jesus came to the rescue of. Bartimaeus was a man with a major, life-long impediment. With one encounter, in one day's time, everything was about to change for the rest of his life.

The story of Bartimaeus is found in Mark 10:46–52 which reads:

> Then they came to Jericho. As Jesus and His disciples, together with a large crowd, were leaving the city, a blind man, Bartimaeus (that is, the son of Timaeus) was sitting by the roadside begging.
>
> When he heard that it was Jesus of Nazareth, he began to shout, "Jesus, Son of David, have mercy on me!"
>
> Many rebuked him and told him to be quiet, but he shouted all the more, "Son of David, have mercy on me!"
>
> Jesus stopped and said, "Call him." So they called to the blind man, "Cheer up! On your feet! He is calling you."

Throwing his cloak aside, he jumped to his feet and came to Jesus.

"What do you want me to do for you?" Jesus asked him.

The blind man said, "Rabbi, I want to see."

"Go," Jesus said, "your faith has healed you." Immediately, he received his sight and followed Jesus along the road.

Here we see Jesus, accompanied by his disciples and a very large crowd, making his way out of the city of Jericho, probably leaving a teaching, preaching, or healing session, and possibly en route to another along with a very large entourage. This was another very busy day in the life of an ultra-busy ministering Messiah. He was a man (and God as well) on a serious, serious mission from God. As Jesus is leaving the city, he comes upon a blind beggar named Bartimaeus, begging for enough to make it through another day.

Bartimaeus, living in first-century Israel, was at the mercy of those who would give him enough to buy food to get him through another day. There was not, in the first-century Israel, social security disability benefits, SSI, and the like. There were no lawyers on TV ready to fight for him in court to win benefits for him. He was on his own, at the mercy of those who would give alms to help out their fellow man.

On top of being poor, a beggar (could you imagine your whole life, day after day after day, having to beg just to make enough to barely scrape by on only to have to go back the following day and do it all over again), what a horrible quality of life. On top of all of that, Bartimaeus was blind as well. That would be doubly horrible. To be blind in Jesus's day would be considered by many to be God's curse on a person because their or their parents' sin.

In John 9:2–3, which speaks of another man who was born blind, Jesus's disciples asked the following question, "His disciples asked Him, 'Rabbi, who sinned, this man or his parents, that he was born blind?' Jesus replied, 'Neither of them did.'"

The point is, many in Jesus's time felt as if the blind had what was coming to them like karma because of their sins. This caused many to respond to a blind beggar with cruelty and judgment, with a he's-getting-what-he-has-coming-to-him kind of mentality instead of with mercy and compassion.

In that respect, some things never seem to change. How many times, in our present day, do people see the poor, the beggar and assume they are drug addicts, they are lazy bums, they are this, they are that when we don't know what their story is? If not for the grace and mercy of God, we may be where they are at ourselves. It is better to not judge and better still to judge with mercy as we would want God to be merciful to us as he judges us.

As Jesus walked by, Bartimaeus cried out in a loud voice for alms, "Can you help a brother out today?" Then one of his fellow beggars who could see, mentioned this was Jesus walking by today. Bartimaeus, realizing this was Jesus walking by, yelled all the louder to get Jesus's attention.

Bartimaeus had heard about Jesus and not only heard of him but believed in him greatly. Bartimaeus knew and believed if he could only get Jesus's attention, Jesus could deliver him from his plight. Bartimaeus believed if he could just get Jesus to stop and recognize his plight, Jesus could deliver him even from something as severe as terminal blindness. Bartimaeus believed that with the Lord, all things are possible to those who believe. Bartimaeus, though a blind beggar, had great faith, belief in Jesus.

How do I know that? By the way he addressed Jesus.

Bartimaeus called out to Jesus in Mark 10:47, "Jesus, Son of David, have mercy on me!"

Again in Mark 10:48, "Bartimaeus said in a loud voice, 'Son of David, have mercy on me!'"

In Jewish culture, referring to Jesus as the Son of David was, in essence, saying, "I believe you are the Messiah, the Son of God, the Savior we have been waiting for." The Israelites believed their Savior, their Messiah, would be a descendant of King David. As Bartimaeus referred to Jesus as Son of David, he was proclaiming his belief on Jesus as Messiah. In the Israelite world where so many doubted

Jesus's claim of being their Messiah, Bartimaeus wholeheartedly and unashamedly believed in Jesus as the Messiah. He may have been physically blind but spiritually, Bartimaeus saw Jesus clearly for who he truly was, the Savior of the world.

Bartimaeus believed and was persistent in crying out to Jesus loudly (Mark 10:48). As he cried out, many rebuked him and told him to be quiet, but he shouted all the more.

Many people, especially one as busy as Jesus, might have walked right on by especially when Bartimaeus started shouting loudly, perhaps thinking Bartimaeus was a crazy man. However, Jesus did not walk on by. Jesus saw Bartimaeus's sincere faith and sincere heart, and it caught his attention. Where others may have seen a poor, worthless (in their eyes) beggar, Jesus saw a precious soul who was made in God's image and who had infinite value.

Friends, this is how Jesus saw Bartimaeus, and this is how the Lord views us as well. Don't mistake how others view us (which may not be so kind and, in some cases, downright vicious and judgmental) with how God views us. God looks at all of us with mercy, with great value to him, and with a heart of redemption. Where others see a loser, a lost cause, an addict, a wretched sinner, Jesus sees you as precious, worth dying for, made in God's image, and longing to redeem and restore. Please, friends, don't mistake the world's view of you with God's view of you, for they could not be more different in so many cases. Jesus has "Come to seek and to save what was lost" (Luke 19:10).

As Jesus heard the heartfelt cries of Bartimaeus, he stopped, laying aside his agenda, his plans. Then his plans and his agenda became solely Bartimaeus who was wholeheartedly seeking after him. Jesus stopped what he was doing and said, "Call him." (Mark 10:49). Those with Bartimaeus said to him, "Cheer up, on your feet! He's calling you."

At this, Bartimaeus threw his cloak aside and ran as fast as he could to Jesus. I imagine Bartimaeus was shocked. The Messiah that he had believed so strongly in and had heard so many great things about, whom he thought he would never personally meet, was right here, right now, calling his name, calling him to himself. Bartimaeus, with great excitement and awe, ran to the Savior.

As he approached Jesus, Jesus asked Bartimaeus something kind of strange, "What do you want me to do for you?" You would think that would be rather obvious given that he was obviously blind. Jesus, as I have observed much in the Gospel, deals much in specifics, not in generalities. He wants to know, as we cry out to him, what we specifically want from him. We would do well to remember that as we approach him in prayer.

In response, Bartimaeus, with great expectation and faith, said, "Rabbi, I want to see." As he uttered these words, I imagine he was thinking to himself, *Could this even be possible? Am I really, truly, having an audience with my Messiah, the Savior of the world? Could this really be the day I have dreamed of my whole life—the day that my blindness turns to sight? Is this really happening, or is this an all-too-wonderful dream?*

And then, he heard the words from the mouth of his wonderful Savior, "Go, your faith has healed you."

Immediately a whole new world opened up to the formerly-blind Bartimaeus. Formerly-blind Bartimaeus now has his vision completely restored, 100 percent, 20-20 vision restored, to a man who had never seen a thing his whole life, a life of darkness restored to living color, now and for the rest of his life. Can you imagine the ecstasy he must have felt? Put yourself in his sandals and imagine the bliss. Blind but now, I see. Hallelujah! Hallelujah! Hallelujah!

Imagine Bartimaeus seeing for the very first time. Imagine the questions he must have asked:

BARTIMAEUS. What is that thing?
ANSWER. That is a flower, those things you have smelled a thousand times.
BARTIMAEUS. They look as good as they smell. How beautiful!
BARTIMAEUS. What are those large things?
ANSWER. Those are cows, horses, and livestock.
BARTIMAEUS. What are those things?
ANSWER. Those are stores, buildings, houses, and a chariot.
BARTIMAEUS. What is that thing with the loud thundering sound?
ANSWER. That is the sea with its waves, crashing on the shore.

BARTIMAEUS. What are those majestic white things way up there?

ANSWER. Those are called clouds up in the sky.

BARTIMAEUS. What are those very unattractive things over there?

ANSWER. Those are men, and you are one of them.

BARTIMAEUS. Oh, I see. And what is that stunningly beautiful creation over there?

ANSWER. Those are women.

BARTIMAEUS. I am really, really liking this seeing thing a lot more now. Boy, oh boy, did God not do a magnificent job creating them. He saved the best for last.

This was the mother of all miracles, performed by a majestic, glorious Savior, Jesus Christ, who was in the miracle-working business then and is in the miracle-working business now as well.

"Jesus Christ is the same yesterday and today and forever" (Hebrew 13:8).

Bartimaeus woke up to what he thought was going to be another wretched day in the life of a blind beggar, but one encounter with Jesus would change the whole trajectory of his life for the rest of his life.

Bartimaeus received the miracle from Jesus Christ that gave him the one thing in this life he desired the most—his eyesight. And what was his response to Jesus as a result of this miracle, the mother of all miracles? Bartimaeus did the wisest thing possible. He did not just receive his miracle and forget about the one who performed it, going on his merry way, forgetting about the one who made him whole. He did not have the mentality of *I've got what I want from God, now I am out of here*. No, Bartimaeus did what all who encounter Jesus should do, and that is to commit their lives to him, fully and for the duration of their lives.

Mark 10:52 says, "Immediately he received his sight and followed Jesus along the road."

We who are wise need to do likewise. We need to not only receive the miracle but all the more embrace personally the miracle worker in a lifelong commitment as well. Wise men and wise women still seek him, and wise men and wise women commit their lives to him once they do find him.

As we conclude, I want to take this from the realm of Bartimaeus into our realm. What can we learn about Jesus ourselves through this powerful story of Bartimaeus? This text teaches us that there is a liberator who is still in the liberating business today.

Friends, if you are a wounded traveler on your journey through this sinful, fallen world where many evil, unfair things happen even to people who are trying to do the right thing, please know Jesus, the ultimate good Samaritan, is looking to help you, to heal and restore you. He is a compassionate Savior who cares deeply, deeply about you whether you know it or not. I challenge you to call out to him, to give him a chance to move upon your life and lead you to a road of redemption. He personally loves you (yes, I said you). He died on the cross for you, and he wants a relationship with you. You may say, "I am not a religious person or at least not very much," or maybe you have only vaguely known of him or have hardly heard of Jesus. I encourage you still to check him out to engage him. I believe if you sincerely do so, you will be blown away by the one you find in him. He longs to make everyone of us new from the inside out, to fill the empty hole in our souls and our hearts. I challenge you to give Jesus a chance. That is exactly what I did as a lost, confused, majorly messed-up, wounded traveler in life in 1990. He gave me a brand-new, born-again, lease on life. I know of countless others who have had the same blessed experience as well. You, like all of us, friend, have nothing to lose and everything to gain. I pray that you will give Jesus a chance. He was truly majestic to Bartimaeus. He is truly majestic to me; and I know, if you open your heart to him, he will prove to be truly majestic to you as well.

He is a master restorer of fallen, broken humanity. This is why he came, and his own personal mission statement tells us as much. It is as follows, found in Luke 4:18–19 which reads:

> The Spirit of the Lord is on me, because
> He has anointed me to preach good news to the
> poor. He has sent me to proclaim freedom for the

prisoners, and recovery of sight for the blind, to
release the oppressed, to proclaim the year of the
Lord's favor.

This mission of Jesus is ongoing. He is still freeing the pris-
oner (whatever your prison is). He is still healing blinded eyes and
blinded hearts as well. He is still releasing the oppressed (from countless oppressions from sinful strongholds and from addictions) from
hopelessness to eternal life and eternal hope. "Christ in us, the hope
of glory" (Colossians 1:27).

Friends, the gospel period we are currently living in is the year
of the Lord's favor. He longs to be merciful, to forgive, to restore,
to reconcile, and to grant you favor with the divine, Almighty God.
Friends, don't let this period of divine favor, this gospel age, pass you
by for, as they say, this is a limited-time offer. One day, it will be one
day too late.

May we all, like Bartimaeus, cry out to Jesus, cry out in faith,
cry out in persistence, cry out in a way that gets his attention; for
one encounter with this glorious Savior can bring deliverance even
from things we thought might be our lifelong lot in life. Bartimaeus
woke up one day blind as blind can be and after his encounter with
Jesus, went on to 20-20 vision for the rest of his days. You may not
be blind (probably most of us aren't), but this same Jesus can set us
free from countless impediments as we look to him in faith. Just like
Bartimaeus, maybe today, this very day, may be your day of liberation. One encounter with Jesus can change the whole trajectory of
your life, now and forever. Amen!

3

A DETERMINED, EXPECTANT FAITH

He said to her, "Daughter, your faith
has healed you. Go in peace and be
freed from your suffering."
—Mark 5:34

As we begin this chapter, I want to begin by exploring together the vital importance of faith. Faith, whether yours today is small, moderate-sized, or very large and growing substantially—regardless of its size, your faith is probably the most precious commodity you possess. Your faith is more important than your money, your possessions, your social status, and a million other things as well.

Why do I say this? Because your faith in God, even if it is not very large yet, is the substance that ushers all into the realm where we can have a life-changing, eternity-changing encounter with the Living God.

Whether you have a great faith in God today or a small faith in God, the Bible says all are given a measure of faith (Romans 12:3, NKJV). The important thing is to use what we do have, and it will grow as we do. Faith is very much like a muscle—the more we use it, exercise it, the more it grows and grows and grows. As we grow in faith (it does not happen overnight), our lives will be greatly enhanced, greatly enriched, and we will continue to see and experience God in very deepening ways.

So in this chapter, I wish to explore: (1) what true faith in God really is; (2) to explore why faith in God is vitally important; and (3) to look at a Bible character who displayed an amazing faith in the Lord and tremendous result of her faith. So here we go:

- What is faith?
- How do we define faith?
- And why is faith so vitally important to us all?

Hebrews 11:1–2, defines faith this way, "Now faith is being sure of what we hope for and certain of what we do not see. This is what the ancients were commended for."

True faith is believing in God, the God of the unseen spiritual realm, and believing in his promises before they come to pass, knowing they will come to pass. The second part of this verse tells us that the great ones in the Bible (here referred to as the ancients) were commended for their great faith in God. Great faith (a rock-solid confidence in God and his promises) was and is the common denominator of all the great ones in the Bible, in the Old and New Testaments.

Why is faith so important? Hebrews 11: 6 says, "And without faith, it is impossible to please God because anyone who comes to Him must believe that He exists and that He rewards those who earnestly seek Him."

Notice here that faith is vitally important, absolutely essential, if we want to connect and please the Living God.

Why? Because it is impossible—not just hard or difficult—but it is impossible to please God without faith. Since this is true (because we believe it by faith), faith is critically important in the life of the believer and also in the life of those who may be seekers but haven't fully committed to the Lord yet. As I mentioned earlier and it bears repeating, faith is the substance that ushers us into the realm where we can have a life-changing, eternity-changing encounter with the Living God.

So if you are a seeker, keep seeking God by faith. If you do, you will find him or rather will be found by God. Jeremiah 29:11–14 says:

> "For I know the plans I have for you," declares the Lord, "plans to prosper you and not harm you, plans to give you a hope and a future.
>
> Then you will call upon Me and come and pray to Me, and I will listen to you.
>
> You will seek Me and find Me when you seek Me with all your heart.
>
> I will be found by you," declares the Lord, "and will bring you back from captivity."
>
> This is God's promise to all who whole-heartedly seek Him.

Without faith, it is impossible to please God nor to truly know God or experience his glory and majesty; but he rewards those who earnestly seek him by faith, and his rewards are absolutely priceless. Without faith, nothing of spiritual substance is possible. But as we believe in God, by faith, all things are possible (Luke 1:37).

As we explore the subject of faith in this chapter, I want to look at a woman in the Scriptures who had an exceptional over-and-above kind of faith. Her story is found in Mark 5:24–34 which reads:

> A large crowd followed and pressed around Him. And a woman was there who had been subject to bleeding for 12 years. She had suffered a great deal under the care of many doctors and spent all she had, yet instead of getting better, she grew worse.
>
> When she heard about Jesus, she came up behind Him in the crowd and touched His cloak because, she thought, "If I touch His clothes, I will be healed."

Immediately, her bleeding stopped and she felt in her body that she was freed from her suffering. At once, Jesus realized that power had gone out from Him. He turned around in the crowd and asked, "Who touched my clothes?"

"You see the people crowding against you," His disciples answered, "and yet you can ask, 'Who touched me?'"

But Jesus kept looking around to see who had done it. Then the woman, knowing what had happened to her, came and fell at his feet and, trembling with fear, told him the whole truth. He said to her, "Daughter, your faith has healed you. Go in peace and be freed from your suffering."

As we dive into this story, I want to share some important observations that will allow us to see the great gravity of her dilemma and to properly understand the majesty of the Lord's deliverance in this woman's life.

1. Here we have a woman with a chronic bleeding disorder, causing her continual bleeding for twelve long years. According to many Bible scholars, this was a uterine or menstrual disorder.

2. On top of the physical pain and discomfort, this woman had suffered a great deal under the care of many doctors. She had gotten a second, third, fourth, and countless opinions from doctor after doctor; and things continued to get worse—not better (Mark 5:26).

3. In addition, this woman had spent all of her money, her resources, every last penny she had, and it did not help her a bit. Actually she had gotten much worse (Mark 5:26).

4. On top of all that, I am sure there was much social ridicule that was heaped on her as well. There were probably cruel people who called her the town sicko or mocked her for

having bloody clothing, people who had no compassion for her horrible plight.

5.   These were just some of the physical and psychological effects. The spiritual implications were even far worse. It is important to understand that she was living in the times of the Mosaic law. Her bleeding issue had horrible consequences for her spiritually as well. If we read this, strictly in the parameters of our culture and not in light of her culture, her times, and her faith, we miss a lot.

Let us examine the spiritual consequences for this woman, living in Israel, living when Jesus was alive, living under Mosaic law. The Levitical law says of a woman who had bleeding disorders, these following laws:

Leviticus 15:19 says, "When a woman has her regular flow of blood, the impurity of her monthly period will last seven days and anyone who touches her will be unclean till evening."

Leviticus 15:25 says, "When a woman has a discharge of blood for many days at a time other than her monthly period or has a discharge that continues beyond her period, she will be unclean as long as she has the discharge, just as in the days of her period.

Lastly, Leviticus 15:27 says, "Whoever touches them will be unclean. He must wash his clothes and bathe with water, and he will be unclean till evening."

Under Jewish law, this woman, because of a condition she had no control over, was ceremonially unclean for twelve long years. Let me break this down for us:

Twelve years is:

- 4,383 days
- 144 months
- 624 weeks
- 105,192 hours
- 6,311,520 minutes
- 378,691,200 seconds

But who is counting, right?

For this long, this woman was ceremonially unclean. She could not worship with the rest of society or be out in public as one unclean. For twelve years, she bore the emotional, psychological, and spiritual baggage (and scars) of being unclean and untouchable. That meant:

- No hugs, no kisses, or any kind of intimacy with her husband (if she had one).
- She could not prepare her family meals as one unclean (if she had a family).
- She could not do housework.
- She could not function as a wife or mom.
- She was isolated in a house, staring at walls for twelve years.

For twelve years, she was, for all intents and purposes, as good as dead.

This was a pretty horrible existence, wouldn't you say? And we think we have problems?

Amazingly, despite all this, she still had hope, and she still had faith.

1. Her faith was a persevering, persistent faith. After all this time and after all she had endured, she still believed. She knew, if she could only touch the Lord Jesus Christ, she would be healed. After all this time, she still trusted God to come through for her. How many of us, honestly, would have kept believing God for deliverance after suffering so long?

   Even if we tried, after a while, most of us would probably give up on believing for a breakthrough after all this time. Not this woman. She had an undying, persevering faith, and she was not going to give up nor accept her present plight as her lot in life. She was not going to give up until her deliverance came. We as believers would do well to follow her persevering example ourselves. Just because you have suffered long does not mean God doesn't have a

33

day of deliverance for you. Maybe, just maybe, your day of breakthrough is just around the corner or this very day. May we, like this great woman of faith, have a persevering, persistent faith.

2. In addition to a persevering, persistent faith, this woman had a determined faith. Hers was an I'm-gonna-get-to-Jesus-no-matter-what-I-have-to-do kind of faith. Jesus was in the middle of a massive crowd of people that almost crushed him (Luke 8:42). How easy, in light of this verse, do you think it would be to get a hand on Jesus? It's hard enough to get through a massive crowd, period, no less to reach the center of attention which was Jesus.

I used to go to Detroit Lions' games at the Pontiac Silverdome, and I remember it being nearly impossible to get to the bathroom or buy concessions at halftime because of the massive crowds. In a massive crowd of people where everyone is crammed together like sardines in a can, it is almost impossible to move no less get to the center of attention. This woman, however, was determined to get to Jesus no matter what, even if it meant getting run over by a massive stampede of humanity. She was determined that no matter what it took to get to him, she was determined to get through to him. She was going to fight with all the strength and energy God gave her to get to Jesus. This woman's faith was a determined faith—a faith that would stop-at-nothing-to-get-to-Jesus kind of faith.

3. Lastly this woman's faith was a get-Jesus's-attention kind of faith, an expectant faith. She knew if she could get through this massive crowd, something miraculous would (not might but would) happen. This woman fought and fought to get through this massive crowd and finally touched Jesus's cloak.

And what happened? The miraculous happened!

Mark 5: 29–31 says:

> Immediately her bleeding stopped and she felt in her body that she was freed from her suffering.
>
> At once Jesus realized that power had gone out from Him. He turned around in the crowd and asked, "Who touched my clothes?"
>
> "You see the people crowding against you," His disciples answered, "and yet you can ask, 'Who touched Me'"
>
> Jesus responded with, "Who touched me?" The disciples replied, "Everyone is touching you, for there is such a large crowd, we are crammed together, and it can't be helped."

Jesus knew this, of course, but he recognized that the touch of this woman was way different from the touch of the crowd. Hers was a touch of pure, unadulterated faith unlike that of the crowd. It was an expectant touch, a touch believing for the miraculous, the supernatural (not a casual touch, simply hoping something would happen). Believe me, friends, when we touch Jesus like this woman touched Jesus, Jesus stands up and takes notice. Jesus takes notice of those who touch him with a touch of true and expectant faith. It gets his attention immediately even in the midst of a massive crowd on a busy day of ministry.

And the result of her faith-filled touch?

Deliverance, relief, ecstasy (over her liberation), for she had received a new lease on life. She was in a state of bliss yet a state of great fear when Jesus said, "Who touched me?"

Why? Because she, with a bleeding issue, was unclean, and she touched Jesus who was clean and holy. This was an Old Testament no-no, and she was fearful of the implications of violating the laws of Moses in this matter. She knew, even though there could be dire consequences, she must confess to Jesus and come clean.

Mark 5:33 says, "Then the woman, knowing what had happened to her, came and fell at His feet and, trembling with fear, told Him the whole truth."

And His response to her?

Anger?

How dare you?

You wicked, sinful, defiled woman?

How could you do such a thing?

No, no, no, and no.

Mark 5:34 says, "He said to her, 'Daughter, your faith has healed you. Go in peace and be freed from your suffering.'"

The cleanness (the holiness) of Jesus overwhelmed the uncleanness of this woman and set her free. The mercy of Jesus triumphed over the judgment of her touching Jesus, as clean, while she was ceremonially unclean. The mercy of Jesus prevailed in her life and set her free. Jesus longs to deliver, to heal, to redeem to set the captive free by his mighty power to set us free.

Jesus says of this:

> "To the Jews who had believed Him, Jesus said, 'If you hold to my teaching, you are really my disciples. Then you will know the Truth, and the Truth will set you free'" (John 8:31–32).

> Jesus replied, "I tell you the truth, everyone who sins is a slave to sin. Now a slave has no permanent place in the family, but a son belongs to it forever. So, if the Son sets you free, you will be free indeed." (John 8:34–36)

Are you free today, friend? If not, God wants to set you free from sin, death, and the grave by the sin-cleansing, soul-cleansing blood of the Lamb, Jesus Christ! The God of infinite grace is looking for you today. If you seek him, you will find him when you seek him with all your heart.

As we close out this chapter, I want to challenge you with these applications from the text of scriptures we explored.

How are you touching Jesus today?

1. Maybe not at all (if not, I challenge you to start)
2. Casually (maybe he will respond, or maybe he won't)
3. Going through the motions (I pray sometimes, it can't hurt)

So many approach Jesus with these mentalities stated above, with too little expectation or possibly wishing something happens but not really expecting something to.

Prayer and approaching Jesus in worship should not be done just simply wishing something will happen or throwing words up in the air (like a Hail-Mary pass) hoping it gets caught. Prayer and worship should be done in faith knowing that, as I engage the Lord in faith and expectancy, he will engage me back in return.

This is what this woman did. She touched Jesus with a powerful touch of faith, and Jesus responded miraculously, changing the whole trajectory of her life for the rest of her life. As a result of her faith-filled touch, she was set free, healed, liberated. The Heavenly One (Jesus) touched the earthly one (this woman), and she was never, ever, ever the same again.

Are you in a desperate situation today like this woman was?

Do you need the heavenly healing from the Savior from heaven, Jesus Christ?

Are you physically broken?

Are you spiritually broken?

Are you emotionally broken?

Do you have a broken heart? Broken by those who you trusted, looked to for guidance and help, for refuge, only to be greatly let down or betrayed?

Do you have a broken life? As one who is a fallen creation living in a fallen world? Are you weary and heavy laden, needing the perfect rest and peace within that can only come from heaven itself?

If so, I have good news for you today! This same Jesus, who healed and restored this severely broken woman who was at the end of her rope, is still in the healing, restoring business for all who look to him in faith.

Hebrews 13:8 says, "Jesus Christ is the same yesterday and today and forever."

What he did then, in this woman's life, he is still doing today for all who touch him in faith.

One encounter with the living, resurrected, soul-saving, life-changing Savior of the world can change your life now and forever.

One encounter with the Living Christ, in one day's time, can change the whole course of our lives, now and forever. Amen!

4

LIBERATION

When they came to Jesus, they saw the
man who had been possessed by the legion
of demons sitting there, dressed, and in
his right mind; and they were afraid.

—Mark 5:15

As we begin this chapter, I want to begin with a sobering truth about life on planet earth and that is, we are in a major war zone whether we realize it or not. Every single human being wakes up every morning, entering into a major, colossal war zone—a war between the forces of God and Jesus and the forces of Satan and his evil spirits. It is a war between the kingdom of God and the kingdom of darkness. We, all humanity, are caught in the middle of this and are greatly affected by these forces.

Though the forces in the spiritual realm are invisible (spiritual in nature and unseen), their effects are certainly not invisible and unseen. We see the carnage all over of people made in God's image (Genesis 1:26–27) who have amazing, almost unlimited potential yet are, in far too many cases, so messed up and broken. This is so heartbreaking to see, and it breaks the heart of God who has made us for so much more than so many of his creation are presently experiencing.

Why does this happen?

Why is it that so many, as children, have great dreams of being policemen, ballerinas, superheroes, even the president of the United

States yet grow up to fall so short of these great dreams? Why is it that so many who have such incredible potential end up addicted to drugs, alcohol, sexual vices, and in prison? What is the root cause of all this dysfunction? Why are lives full of chaos, unfulfilled potential, brokenness, emptiness, etc., etc.?

The root cause of all these broken dreams, broken lives, this sense of *I've lost my way* is twofold. The first cause is the effects of sin upon lives of such great potential and made in God's image; and the second cause is Satan and his evil forces, plunging humanity into the depths of despair they were never meant to go to. Jesus tells us about Satan, that this thief comes only to steal and kill and destroy (John 10:10). Boy, is he good at his craft! He has successfully wreaked havoc on countless lives and has so many in a state of emptiness, frustration, and despair. All of us, myself certainly included, have been majorly affected by the destructive power of Satan. He is certainly at work—fast and furious—in his destructive work down here on earth.

While this is true, praise God, this is not the end of the story. While Satan comes to steal and kill and destroy, Jesus said in the second part of John 10:10, "I have come that they may have life, and life to the full." This second part of John 10:10 in the KJV, Jesus said, "I am come that they might have life and that they might have it more abundantly." So we are caught in the middle between a real devil who is working relentlessly to destroy us and a very real Savior, Jesus Christ, who wants to save us, restore us, and give us life to the full, an abundant life in him. We are caught in a colossal, very real, spiritual war zone, and that is the human story. We must all decide for ourselves which side we want to join forces with. This choice will either make us or break us.

In this chapter, we are going to look at a man who was caught up about as deeply as any human could be in the destructive power of Satan and who was, by the power of Jesus, about to receive the mother of all miraculous deliverances.

This man's story is found in Mark 5:1–20 which reads:

> They went across the lake to the region of
> the Gerasenes. When Jesus got out of the boat, a

man with an evil spirit came from the tombs to meet Him. This man lived in the tombs and no one could bind him any more, not even with a chain.

For he had often been chained hand and foot, but he tore the chains apart, and broke the irons on his feet. No one was strong enough to subdue him. Night and day among the tombs and in the hills he would cry out and cut himself with stones.

When he saw Jesus from a distance, he ran and fell on his knees in front of him. He shouted at the top of his voice, "What do you want with me, Jesus, Son of the Most High God? Swear to God that you won't torture me!"

For Jesus had said to him, "Come out of this man, you evil spirit!"

Then Jesus asked him, "What is your name?" "My name is Legion" he replied, "for we are many." And he begged Jesus again and again not to send them out of the area.

A large herd of pigs was feeding on the nearby hillside.

The demons begged Jesus, "Send us among the pigs; allow us to go into them."

He gave them permission, and the evil spirits came out and went into the pigs. The herd, about two thousand in number, rushed down the steep bank into the lake and were drowned.

Those tending the pigs ran off and reported this in the town and countryside, and the people went out to see what had happened.

When they came to Jesus, they saw the man who had been possessed by the legion of demons sitting there, dressed and in his right mind, and they were afraid.

Those who had seen it told the people what had happened to the demon-possessed man and told about the pigs as well.

Then the people began to plead with Jesus to leave this region.

As Jesus was getting into the boat, the man who had been demon possessed begged to go with Him.

Jesus did not let him but said, "Go to your family and tell them how much the Lord has done for you and how He has had mercy on you."

So, the man went away and began to tell in the Decapolis how much Jesus had done for him. And all the people were amazed."

As we consider this text, I want to begin with a few questions for us to strongly consider and to answer honestly.

1. Have you ever looked at another person and thought that person is too far gone? That person is a lost cause? Irredeemable (please answer honestly)?
2. Have you ever looked at another and thought that person is too addicted—no one could ever get them free (too addicted to drugs, alcohol, gambling, sexual immorality, or to this vice or that vice)? They are enslaved and too far gone?
3. Have you ever written anybody off?

Or maybe you, yourself, have felt, "I am in too much bondage, and I can never break free of this bondage or this addiction" or been told this by another.

If you have ever thought this or felt this way about yourself or another, I want to greatly challenge your thinking in light of what we just read.

What I mean is this: Can you get any more messed up, any more enslaved, any more demon-possessed, seemingly any more too far gone than the man we just read about here? Think about this.

This man:

> "Lived in the tombs, and not even chains could bind him" (Mark 5:3).

> "He was chained hand and foot, and he had iron shackles on his feet and yet he tore them off and broke them" (Mark 5:4).

> "He lived in the tombs and hills and would cry out and cut himself with stones violently" (Mark 5:5).

This man said he had a legion of demons living in him (Mark 5:9). A legion was the largest unit of the Roman Army, consisting of 3,000–6,000 soldiers. This man literally had thousands of demons possessing him.

Again can you get any more messed up, seemingly any more too far gone than this man was?

If anyone was too far gone, it would have been this guy; but as we read in this text, he wasn't too far gone. Neither are you (if you feel that way), and neither are any others!

Why? Because there is a Savior named Jesus Christ who can do anything, who has more than sufficient power to save, to deliver, to liberate, to set free from bondage no matter who you are and no matter how enslaved you may think you/others are!

I believe this text tells us that every person can find spiritual liberation in Christ.

How? By removing the boundaries we may have on God.

Boundary Number 1: Unbelief in the Almighty Power of God

We have already established how demon-possessed, how enslaved this man was to very powerful demonic forces (and believe me, they are extremely powerful) as witnessed by the grip these demons had on this man. This passage tells us no chain, no shackles could bind him, nor could any human being stand against him. He was filled to overflowing with demons.

That being true, notice how this demon-possessed man, who was overwhelming everyone and everything else, responded to Jesus.

Mark 5:6–7 says:

> When he saw Jesus from a distance, he ran and fell on his knees in front of Him. He shouted at the top of his voice, "What do you want with me, Jesus, Son of the Most High God?" Swear to God that you won't torture me.

Mark 5:10 says, "And he (the demon-possessed man) begged Jesus again and again not to send them out of the area."

Mark 5:12 says, "The demons begged Jesus, 'Send us among the pigs. Allow us to go into them,'"

Did you catch all that?

This demon-possessed man (and the demonic forces within him) knew undeniably who the boss was, who the greater was and who the lesser was. These demons that had overpowered all the rest knew, as soon as Jesus walked onto the scene, that they were no match for Jesus and fell at his feet, begging for mercy. They knew that they were no match, none whatsoever, for Jesus. They knew their power was nothing in comparison to the power of Jesus.

The demons know, beyond a shadow of a doubt, the almighty power of Jesus. But what about us? Why do we doubt?

Sadly it seems that the demons have far greater faith in God, in Jesus, than we do. They understand that no force, no matter how powerful, can stand against the power of Jesus. It is not even close.

What would happen, people of God, seeker of God, if we started believing in the power of Jesus, like these demons did here, in our own personal lives? What if we believed in Jesus and the almighty, matchless power with unwavering faith? I believe we (myself certainly included) would experience a transformation and liberation within that would make us far more effective servants of Jesus and servants in God's kingdom.

Do we (be honest now) believe our circumstances, the demons that oppose us, our trials, are bigger than the power of Jesus? Or do we truly believe that the power of Jesus is greater than anything or anyone who opposes us, bar none?

Do we, as it is said, tell God how big our trial, our mountain, our Goliath, is? Or do we tell our trial, our mountain, our Goliath how big our God is?

I pray that we, as God's people or seekers of God, will grab hold of and not let go of the faith, the belief in the omnipotent Savior, Jesus Christ, we see displayed in this story of the demon-possessed man. May we all know and believe in the all-powerful, all-sufficient Savior who set this man free and can do the same for us.

May our faith echo the faith of the prophet Jeremiah who said in Jeremiah 32:17, "Ah, Sovereign Lord, you have made the heavens and the earth by your great power and outstretched arm. Nothing is too hard for you."

Luke 1:37 says, "For nothing is impossible with God."

This is the absolute truth, may we stand unwavering in our devotion and faith in this almighty, all-sufficient God and Savior who is unmatched in divine power. Amen!

I believe also that this text tells us that every person can find spiritual liberation in Christ.

How? By removing the boundaries we may have on God.

Boundary Number 2: Unbelief in the Sovereignty of Jesus, the Sovereignty of God

What do I mean by the sovereignty of Jesus and sovereignty of God?

Sovereignty means that God is the ultimate authority. It is knowing that God has final say.

Notice the following verses from our text: Mark 5:10 says, "The demons begged Jesus, 'Send us among the pigs; allow us to go into them.' He gave them permission and the evil spirits came out and went into the pigs."

Here we see these demons begging Jesus for things because they understood he (not they) had final say. He had the ultimate authority. He was/is sovereign over all. If this wasn't true, these demons would have done as they pleased. In Mark 5:13, it says, "He gave them permission."

This greater authority gives permission to the lesser. The higher authority gives authority to the lesser authority, and not the other way around.

As Jesus spoke the word of deliverance by the power of God, this legion (not just one or two but a legion) of demons were instantly cast out of this human into a herd of pigs which proceeded to rush down this steep bank into the lake to drown themselves.

Can you imagine being a witness to such an event?

It would have been both amazing and also hair-raising simultaneously.

One minute, you have this demon-possessed man breaking chains, breaking shackles, possibly foaming at the mouth, possibly spewing out profane, evil words from his mouth (which is what I imagine the dialect of the demon-possessed would be like)—a stark-raving demon-possessed lunatic. This man was the personification of pure evil, the embodiment of hell itself in human form, having lost all control of himself, a puppet of the legion of demons that possessed him. He was one that anyone in their right mind would not want to be anywhere around.

Then Jesus shows up and these demons in this man, recognizing Jesus for who he was/is, the omnipotent Son of God, beg to be sent into this herd of pigs. Jesus gives them the go ahead and 2,000 pigs, invaded by the demons, rush down the steep bank into the lake.

I can't imagine seeing such a sight. Imagine you and your family, taking a family on a first-century family vacation to the Decapolis and all of a sudden, you spot this event in real time and yell, "Dude! Check this out! Whoa! Look at this herd of pigs, plunging to their death. Quick, record this! This will cause our Facebook page to blow up more than ever before." After this is all over, we would stand there, awestruck, as we process all that we just beheld, and the wife wanders in disbelief at what she just saw and how her husband, in the rush of all that just happened, called her "dude," lol!

Okay, back to the serious stuff for just a little bit longer.

Notice, in this story, what the demons, which possessed this man, begged Jesus for repeatedly?

Mark 5:10 says, "He begged Jesus again and again not to send them out of the area."

Why would he/they ask for such a thing?

What made these demons want so desperately to stay in this particular area?

I am pretty sure I know the answer to that, and this is godlessness. The area of the Decapolis was a very godless area, and the demons were thriving there as a result of the blatant godlessness. This was an area that had rejected God, rejected Jesus; and as a result, Satan and his demons were having virtually free reign. Then we wonder why unspeakable, evil things happen when Jesus and his Gospel had been evicted. That's the root cause. This is why we see acts of pure, unspeakable evil even in places that were, at one time, safe havens. You evict the light, then darkness reigns supreme. You evict godliness and good, then evil reigns supreme. To reject God, Jesus, is to open the door for wickedness and evil to prevail.

While wickedness reigns where godliness and goodness are absent, the principle, fortunately, works the other way as well.

Where Christ is wholeheartedly embraced, the power of Satan and wickedness cannot thrive or prevail. Satan does not thrive, Satan does not want to be where godliness, righteousness, love for Jesus, and hatred toward sin reign supreme (notice I did not say hatred towards sinners but hatred toward sin, and there is a difference). True love for God should, by nature, produce a hatred toward sin (our own and sin in others as well); but true love for God should also, by nature, cause us to love others more and more and more despite how sinful they may be. We are called, as Christian believers, to love everyone deeply, sinner or saint, but not to love sin. We hate sin in ourselves and others because we hate the destructive effect sin has on us and others and don't want to see anyone destroyed by it.

Bottom lines on this: You want Satan and his forces to flee (I would hope we would all say yes, absolutely yes) and then close the door of your heart and to our society to Satan by wholeheartedly embracing Jesus, the gospel of light which dispels the darkness, and dedicate your life, your heart, your being to Jesus, living for and in him. Willful sin opens the door for Satan and his forces. True godly sorrow and repentance and embracing Jesus slam the doors on Satan and his forces. We as individuals and as a society need to put up a "No Vacancy" sign to Satan by embracing Jesus and his Holy Word.

The question for all of us, in light of this, is: where are you in this equation?

Are you embracing Christ and his gospel?

Or are you living a purely secular and godless life right now?

And where are we as a society in this equation? Are we a society plagued by apostasy (meaning a nation/a people moving swiftly away from God)? Or are we a society/a people moving rapidly toward God and his Son, Jesus Christ?

This people, this community of the Decapolis, after seeing or hearing about the deliverance Jesus brought to this demoniac, this amazing, miraculous act, asked Jesus to leave their area. They evicted the liberator, the miracle worker, the one who sets the enslaved free. To me, this is absolutely shocking and majorly skewed beyond belief.

Mark 5:17 says, "Then the people began to plead with Jesus to leave their region."

Sometimes I feel, in this present world we are living in, that we have embraced the mentality of the Decapolis—go away Jesus and take your church and your gospel with you.

Friends, nation, fellow citizens in this generation, I urge us to reconsider this mentality, for this mindset, either in individuals or a nation, never, ever, ever ends well.

So may we do what the epistle writer James says in James 4:7 which reads, "Submit yourselves then to God. Resist the devil, and he will flee from you."

Jesus is a gentleman. He does not force his way in. He comes to us as we, from our hearts, welcome him in. I pray we would, as individuals, as a society, and as a world, throw open the doors of our hearts to the Savior of the world. By doing so, we find abundance in Christ and liberation from hell's power which is what happened to the formerly demon-possessed, demon-enslaved, self-mutilating demoniac. He was totally set free by the power of Jesus.

Mark 5:15 says, "When they came to Jesus, they saw this man who had been possessed by the legion of demons sitting there, dressed, and in his right mind; and they were afraid."

Mark 5: 18–20 says:

> As Jesus was getting into the boat, the man who had been demon possessed begging to go with Him. Jesus did not let him go but said, "Go home to your family and tell them how much the Lord has done for you and how He had mercy on you." So, the man went away and began to tell in the Decapolis how much Jesus had done for him.

This man went from (before Christ):

- Living in tombs (Mark 5:2).
- Filled with a legion of demons (Mark 5:9).
- Breaking chains (Mark5:3).
- Breaking iron shackles (Mark 5:4).
- No one strong enough to subdue or control him (Mark 5:4).
- Crying out with evil shrieks (Mark 5:5).
- Self mutilating, self-destructive behavior (Mark 5:5).
- Fearful of Jesus (Mark 5:7),
- Fearful of divine judgment (Mark 5:7.

To (after Christ):

- Dressed (Mark 5:15).
- In his right mind (Mark 5:15).
- Eager to follow Jesus (Mark 5:18).
- Liberated (Mark 5:15).

- Filled with a divine purpose to be an ambassador for Christ, carrying his message to others (Mark 5:19).

A brand-new man, a brand-new creation in Christ (2 Corinthians 5:17).

A man with a brand-new spiritual identity in God's family (2 Corinthians 5:17).

This man woke up an out-of-control, enslaved-by-demons, self-destructive, self-mutilating embodiment of evil. In one day's time, with one very real encounter with Jesus, everything changed for this man for the rest of his life.

From slavery to freedom.

From self-destructive behavior to wholeness.

From recklessness to divine purpose.

From the lordship of Satan to the Lordship of Christ.

From lost to found.

From emptiness to abundance in Christ.

Friends, seekers of Christ, this man's story can be your story as well. No matter how far gone you think you are or think others are, there is no one, absolutely no one that Christ cannot or will not save if we/they open our hearts to him. He was in the spiritual-saving, spiritual-liberating business then; and he is in the spiritual-saving, liberation business now. No demon in hell, no matter how powerful, can overcome what he determines to do.

Jesus's modus operandi is this: "For the Son of Man came to seek and to save what was lost" (Luke 19:10).

Jesus has come to set us free!

John 8:31–32 says of this, "To the Jews who had believed Him, Jesus said, 'If you hold to my teaching, you are really my disciples. Then you will know the truth, and the truth will set you free.'"

John 8:36 says, "So if the Son sets you free, you will be free indeed."

This is Jesus's desire for all mankind, not just some elites or a select few but for all, including you, my friend. No matter what you are up against, no matter how many demons you are battling with today, if you will turn your heart to Jesus, he will set you free.

I unapologetically close with this proclamation to you, to all of humanity:

> Jesus Christ has come to set us free!
> Jesus Christ has come to set us free!
> Jesus Christ has come to set you free!

Hallelujah! Hallelujah! And hallelujah! To Jesus, the Divine Liberator, now and forevermore!

In one day's time, with one real encounter with Jesus Christ, we can be set free, now and forever. Amen! And amen!

CHAPTER

5

WHAT IS A SEEKER?

"But Zacchaeus stood up and said to the
Lord, 'Look, Lord! Here and now I give
half of my possessions to the poor and, if
I have cheated anyone out of anything, I
will pay back four times the amount.'"
—Luke 19:8

In this chapter, we will be exploring what it means to be a seeker and why many become seekers in the first place. We will also look at the life of another biblical seeker named Zacchaeus and how he ended up finding what (and who) he was seeking for his whole life.

As we begin, I want to begin with the obvious question and that is: what is a seeker?

A seeker, in the sense of the word I want to address, is: (1) One who is trying to figure out what this life is supposed to be all about. (2) Secondly what is my purpose, if I even have one, in the grand scheme of life (do I exist for a purpose, or do I just exist to exist with no set role in the grand scheme of life?). (3) Seekers are those who realize there's a missing piece and missing peace within, and they are seeking to find out the source of the missing piece and missing peace. Seekers sense deep within that there is something or someone missing, and they are seeking for what that something or who that someone really is.

The second question piggybacks off the first, and that is: why do many become seekers in the first place?

I believe that the reason many become seekers is that, at some point in their lives, they have realized that there's got to be more to life than just merely existing for no set purpose or no good reason. Seekers realize that there must be a reason for their being here in life, a purpose that they are called to fulfill, and they are seeking to find out what that role in the world is. Lastly I believe the reason many become seekers is that they feel a void, a vacuum, a hole in the soul and are looking for what it is or who it is that can fill that empty place within. Seekers are longing for inward contentment and a sense that I am accomplishing what I was created to accomplish in the very depths of their being.

In this chapter, we will be exploring the life of Zacchaeus, a man who was deeply seeking for this missing piece and the missing peace within and where he found the answer he was looking for. Zacchaeus's story was quite unlike those we have thus far explored (the paralytic, blind Bartimaeus, the woman with the issue of blood, and the demoniac) for on the surface of things, he seemed to be living the dream, a charmed life if you will. Those we have explored in prior chapters had major impediments, handicaps, and strongholds in their lives. Zacchaeus, however, on the surface, looked like he had everything together, living a lifestyle of prosperity that many would long to have.

Our world, especially in a prosperous nation like America, is filled with many Zacchaeus's, those who may look on the surface like they are living the dream but in their heart of hearts, are inwardly miserable. They are unfulfilled, empty, and feeling lost. How else do you explain celebrities, business executives, insanely wealthy and prosperous people who sometimes take their own lives or are severely addicted to drugs, alcohol, or various other vices? I am not making light of their difficulties, pains, and struggles but quite simply pointing out that if money, prosperity, or fame can fulfill the inner longings within, they of all people would be the most content, happy, fulfilled people on the planet earth; and that is very often not the case.

With that, I want us to look together at the story of Zacchaeus and see what we can learn in our search for the inner piece and the inner peace from his life. His story is found in Luke 19:1–10 which reads:

> Jesus entered Jericho and was passing through. A man was there by the name of Zacchaeus; he was a chief tax collector and was wealthy. He wanted to see who Jesus was but, being a short man, he could not because of the crowd. So he ran ahead and climbed a sycamore-fig tree to see him since Jesus was coming that way. When Jesus reached the spot, he looked up and said to him, "Zacchaeus, come down immediately. I must stay at your house today."
>
> So he came down at once and welcomed Him gladly. All the people saw this and began to mutter, "He has gone to be the guest of a sinner." But Zacchaeus stood up and said to the Lord, "Look, Lord! Here and now I give half of my possessions to the poor, and, if I cheated anybody out of anything, I will pay back four times the amount."
>
> Jesus said to him, "Today salvation has come to this house because this man, too, is a son of Abraham. For the Son of Man came to seek and to save what was lost."

In this story, we see Zacchaeus was a very wealthy man (Luke 19:2), one who was very financially prosperous as a chief tax collector. Zacchaeus was in a deep search for Jesus (Luke 19:3–4) and as a chief tax collector was deeply unpopular among the Israelites (Luke 19:7). Though deeply unpopular with the people, Jesus called Zacchaeus unto himself.

To properly grasp the meaning of this story of Zacchaeus, it's important to understand some key points in this story.

The first point is the nature of Zacchaeus's profession as a chief tax collector, the source of his great wealth. This profession, though very prosperous, made him the object of great scorn and hatred among the Israelite people. In Israelite culture, tax collectors were deeply hated and chief tax collectors were hated even more because they made great wealth at the expense of the common people and poor people in Israel.

The Israelites despised tax collectors of which Zacchaeus was chief because they were agents of the Roman Empire who ruled over Israel during Jesus's lifetime even though it was not their country. The Roman Empire extorted much money from the Israelis and all the nations under their control to fund their powerful empire. The Jews hated this because: (1) The Roman taxation was exorbitant (way, way too high). (2) Their tax money was used to further the cause of a secular government and to pagan gods, not the cause of Israel and the Israeli's God.

How many of us would like that? To have a foreign ruling power come into your sovereign nature, extort money from your nation and people, and use it to further their nation, not yours. The Israelite hatred of such things was totally justified.

The tax collectors and chief tax collectors were Jewish by birth but coconspirators with Rome to extort money from their own countrymen to make Rome and themselves very rich in the process. Zacchaeus was a chief tax collector and probably a very unethical, corrupt one as well based on how much he was despised by his fellow countrymen. Zacchaeus was the head of a gang of traitors, cheaters, professionals at extorting money from the poor and making themselves rich in the process.

This is who Zacchaeus was on the surface; but below the surface, Zacchaeus was a seeker, one looking for a better way. Zacchaeus, though very wealthy and prosperous financially, was, in his soul, realizing that all this outward wealth and the unethical nature in which he accumulated this wealth was very empty and unfulfilled. Zacchaeus, unbeknownst to the crowd, was looking for a whole new direction in life. Zacchaeus had grown tired and weary of his present way of life and was seeking a new way of living. Maybe some of you reading these pages right now can relate to where Zacchaeus was, for you are in the same place.

If you, like Zacchaeus, are in this place, looking for a new direction, the good news is the Lord sees your heart. This seeking was going on within the heart of Zacchaeus. The common people could not see that; but fortunately, Jesus could. The common people only saw in Zacchaeus an evil, corrupt person who would never change; but Jesus saw a sinner seeking a new direction within. The common people only saw the present Zacchaeus. Jesus, however, saw the wonderful person he could become once Jesus got hold of his heart. Friends, seekers, please don't mistake how God views you with how people do which can be polar opposites. People see you for where you are today. God looks at what you can become as you embrace the Lord in your heart.

Notice how, in this story of Zacchaeus, when everyone else was pushing Zacchaeus away, Jesus welcomed him in. Jesus said, "Zacchaeus, come down immediately. I am coming to your house today," and welcomed him gladly (Luke 19:5– 6). Contrast that with what the common people were thinking. The people saw this, started muttering, "He is going to be a guest of this vile sinner" (Luke 19:7). Jesus welcomed Zacchaeus gladly. The common people, however, were repulsed with how Jesus embraced this sinner. It's important to remember, man looks at the surface level, but God sees the heart. Man sees the outer, present person, but God sees the heart of a seeker and what you can become, future tense, as the Lord comes into your heart. Men might be naysayers, but the Lord can be your cheerleader who believes greatly in what you can become in him.

Look at what happened, almost immediately, in Zacchaeus's life as he received the embrace and acceptance of the Lord. He was a changed man from within, and this inward change brought outward change. "Zacchaeus stood up and said, 'Look, Lord! Here and now I give half my possessions to the poor. And, if I have cheated anybody out of anything, I will pay back four times the amount'" (Luke 19:8).

Talk about repentance, a total change of heart. Zacchaeus was not only sorry for what he had been but wanted to make amends with anyone he offended, much to the delight of Jesus and the shock of the naysayers. This was a quick, radical transformation as Jesus embraced this lost, seeking sinner with a loving embrace. In one encounter, in one day's time with the living Lord, Zacchaeus's trajectory of life was changed forever.

Look at Jesus's response to this:

"Jesus said to him, 'Today salvation has come to this house because this man, too, is a son of Abraham. For the Son of Man came to seek and to save what was lost'" (Luke 19:9–10).

Zacchaeus was a truly changed man with one very real touch from heaven upon his heart.

Zacchaeus went from:

- Seeker to finder (he found the Lord, and the Lord found him)
- Corrupt to made right (longing to make amends for wrongdoing)
- Greedy to generous (I'll give half of what I own to the poor and pay back those I have wronged four times as much)
- From lost in sin to saved from sin (salvation has come to this house)
- From a child of the world to child of God
- From unbeliever to redeemed believer (a child of Abraham)

Scripture says of this inside-out change these words, found in 2 Corinthians 5:17–19:

> Therefore, if anyone is in Christ, he is a new creation; the old has gone, the new has come!
> All this is from God who reconciled us to Himself through Christ and gave us the ministry of reconciliation; That God was reconciling the world to Himself in Christ, not counting men's sins against them.

This inside-out change, like we see here in the story of Zacchaeus, is very real and very transformative, a modern-day mother-of-all miracles for all those who experience it. Jesus refers to this inside-out change as being born again or born from above (John 3:3– 7). The great news of the Bible is that God, through Christ, longs to save and give brand-new inside-out life to all seekers including you (if you have never experienced God's salvation). This is the very reason Jesus came to this earth—to save, redeem, and transform lost sinners into brand-new creations, sons and daughters of God Most High. Zacchaeus's experience can be your personal experience as well. How do I know this? Because the story of Zacchaeus tells us in verse 10, "For the Son of Man came to seek and to save what was lost." This God of all grace is looking for you like he was seeking out Zacchaeus.

For the rest of this chapter, I want to take this story of Zacchaeus from his realm into ours. In other words, what does Zacchaeus's story have to say to us personally about God? What does this story say to all seekers? I want to share some observations.

First of all, the soul, the inner man, has great longings and hunger.

Seekers, as I mentioned at the beginning of this chapter, become seekers because they realize that there is a vacuum, a void, a hole in the soul if you will. There is a deep longing within, an empty space that longs to be filled and fulfilled! God created the soul this way. This longing within is our soul longing to be reconnected to the God who gave it to us in the first place. If you are a seeker of the missing piece and missing peace, this inward longing can only be filled and fulfilled with the God who created us in his image with spiritual longings.

David the psalmist speaks of this deep, internal longing this way in Psalm 42:1–2. "As the deer pants for streams of water, so my soul pants for you, O God. My soul thirsts for God, for the living God, when can I go and meet with God?"

> Why are you downcast, O my soul? Why
> so disturbed within me? Put your hope in God,
> for I will yet praise Him, my Savior and my God.
> My soul is downcast within me; therefore, I will

remember you from the land of the Jordan, the
heights of Hermon, from Mount Mizar. Deep
calls to deep, in the roar of your waterfalls. (Psalm
42:5–7)

Our souls, our inner being, hungers and thirsts to reconnect
with God within. The depths of our being (deep calls to deep) longs
to connect with the depths of God's being. Soul to soul, deep calling
to deep. In God alone can our internal soul find comfort, the love it
longs for, the fulfillment and contentment it truly longs for.

This is why Zacchaeus, though filthy rich, was internally dis-
satisfied. This is why many of those who have so much of outward
possessions (fame, fortune, beautiful mate/spouse, worldly power,
talent that surpasses the multitudes, etc., etc.) are still miserable,
unfulfilled, and empty within. They still haven't found what they are
looking for even though they have infinitely much more than 99.9
percent of everyone else.

Friends, seekers of God, nothing—and I mean absolutely nothing—can take the place of God in our lives, in our inner man, our
soul. The depths of our being (our soul) longs for the depths of God,
and nothing else and no one else can fill that role. But praise God;
God, through Jesus Christ his Son, can fill the deep longings of the
soul. Jesus said of those who wholeheartedly seek him and his righteousness, these words in Matthew 5:6, "Blessed are those who hunger and thirst for righteousness for they will be filled."

In Christ, our internal hunger and thirst can find fulfilment
and satisfaction. Our soul can be filled by the one it longs for most.

This Jesus Christ was the one Zacchaeus found (or was found
by) and was the treasure that he had been searching for all along. This
was my story as well. I was a seeker from about the age of fifteen to
the age of twenty-three, seeking diligently for the missing piece and
missing peace. I had great longing within but just didn't know what
or who I was longing for. I experimented with many things I now
regret, trying to fulfill this internal longing within. I even was a little
bit religious but really did not personally know or embrace Jesus in
my heart. Finally in the fall of 1990, I cried out to Jesus wholeheart-

edly and with an all-in approach and was born again. In Jesus, I found the treasure, the missing piece and peace, my soul longed for. I have never been the same since. Jesus is more wonderful, beautiful, internally magnificent than I could ever describe to you. He was, in 1990 when I first met him personally and twenty-eight years later, is all I could ever dream for as well.

In the beginning of the chapter, I shared how seekers are those who are trying to figure out what this life is really supposed to be all about. The story of Zacchaeus, as well as all the rest of the Bible, Old and New Testaments, teaches us that life that is truly life comes from connecting with God relationally. We are created by God to be in a soul-to-soul, our-spirit-with-God's-Spirit, intimate relationship with God through Jesus Christ, humanity's Savior and Redeemer.

Both the Old Testament and New Testament teach us that the first and greatest commandment is to love God with all of our being. Jesus Christ said, quoting Deuteronomy 6:5, in Matthew 22:37–40:

> Love the Lord your God with all your heart and with all your soul and with all of your mind. This is the first and greatest commandment.
>
> And the second is like it. Love your neighbor as yourself.
>
> All the law and prophets hang on these two commandments.

These two commandments explain our reason for being, for why we exist—to love God from the depths of our being and to be loved by God in return with a love that is beyond comprehension and words to describe.

Psalm 103:11 says of God's love, "For as high as the heavens are above the earth, so great is His love for those who fear Him."

Can anyone accurately measure how high the farthest reaches of the galaxies are above the earth? That's how limitless and measureless God's love is for those who fear him and follow him.

The Apostle Paul says of this limitless love of God in Christ with these words in Ephesians 3:17–19:

> And I pray that you, being rooted and estab-
> lished in love, may have power together with all
> the saints to grasp how wide and long and high
> and deep is the love of Christ, And to know this
> love that surpasses knowledge that you may be
> filled with the measure of all the fullness of God.

God's love is limitless, vast, and incomprehensible for all his redeemed children, and it will never end.

Psalm 103:17 says of the endless love of God, "But from ever-lasting to everlasting the Lord's love is with those who fear Him and His righteousness with their children's children."

This limitless love of God is poured into our hearts and lives so we may pour out that same kind of love to our neighbors thus ful-filling the second half of the great commandment. God created us to know him relationally and to love and be loved by him relationally. This is at the core of the meaning of life and why we exist. Paul says, of this great God who created us, in Acts 17:28, "For in Him we live and move and have our being."

Along with this question of "Why do I exist?" many seekers also want to know "Do I have a purpose?" in the grand scheme of life. God's Word speaks strongly to that as well. By learning these truths of Scripture, it adds great clarity to our lives.

God's Word speaks of a God who created us (you, me, all of us). God created us, first of all, on purpose.

How can I say that?

How do I know that?

God's Word speaks of a God who created us and knows us inti-mately well.

Psalm 139:13–16 says:

> For you created my inmost being; you knit
> me together in my mother's womb. I praise you

because I am fearfully and wonderfully made;
your works are wonderful; I know that full well.

My frame was not hidden from you when I
was made in the secret place, when I was woven
together in the depths of the earth. Your eyes saw
my unformed body. All the days ordained for me
were written in your book before one of them
came to be.

God was there at our conception, (1) creating our inmost being;
(2) knitting us together in our mother's womb as fearfully and wonderfully made creations. We were created on purpose by the hands of
the Almighty God who knows us intimately well.

Secondly God has also created us, every single one of us, for a
purpose, a good purpose, in the grand scheme of this life.

How can I say that?

How do I know this?

For God's Word tells us so. Jeremiah 29:11 says: "'For I know
the plans I have for you,' declares the Lord, 'plans to prosper you and
not to harm you, plans to give you hope and a future.'"

The Apostle Paul says in Ephesians 2:10, "For we are God's
workmanship, created in Christ Jesus to do good works, which God
prepared in advance for us to do."

We are not, as some would have us think, cosmic accident or
humans who exist for no good reason. We are created on purpose, by
God, for a great divine purpose that will prosper us and not harm us,
that will give us hope and a future.

God has created us to love him and to be greatly loved by him
with a love that is limitless and endless in duration. He (God) has
created us on purpose for a purpose.

Friends, seekers of God, your life matters more than you could
ever fathom. Your life matters so much to the God who created you,
who loves you and longs for you to know him (if you do not already).
Your life purpose is vitally important in what God wants to do in this
world for such a time as this.

If you are a seeker, seek God and his Son, Jesus Christ. In him, you will find, like Zacchaeus, life that is truly life and truly abundant. The good news, if you are seeking him, is you can know he is seeking you as well.

> "For the Son of Man came to seek and to save what was lost" (Luke 19:10).

In all these lives we have explored so far, there is a common theme.

In one day's time, with one encounter with the Lord, the whole trajectory of their lives was forever changed.

Dear friend and seeker, that can be your story as well. Today God may start the miracle in your life that changes the trajectory of your whole life too. Try Jesus. You have nothing to lose and everything to gain.

It is my earnest prayer that God will do a right-now and forevermore miracle in all of your lives.

In one day's time, with one encounter with the Living God, everything and I mean everything, can change forever.

6

THE UNLOVED BECAME
THE DEARLY BELOVED

Jesus answered her, "If you knew the gift
of God and Who it is that asks you for a
drink, you would have asked Him and He
would have given you living water."

As we begin this chapter, I have some questions I want to ask you personally, and I want you to answer the questions for yourself very honestly.

The first question is: do you feel that God likes, or loves, others more than you?

If you answered yes, I have a second question which is: Do you believe that way because others have told you that or strongly implied that that was the case? Do you just feel that way but have no concrete basis for that belief? Do you feel that way because you have sinned a lot? Guess what, friend! We all have! Romans 3:23 says, "For all have sinned and fall short of the glory of God."

The reason I ask and I challenge you to think deeply about the above question is because I believe there is a deceptive false narrative sweeping through our land. That false narrative is that God couldn't love me as much as others or at all (for some) because of this, that, or the other reasons. We have embraced in our minds—God couldn't love me because I was born on the wrong side of the tracks; God couldn't love me because I am poor; I am a nobody; I am not one of the beautiful people. These are thoughts that run daily through minds of multitudes of people, possibly including you.

So many of those thoughts convince us we are unworthy of God's love, but that is true of all humanity, not just for some. We all, because of sin, are unworthy of God's great love, but God gives it to us anyway as we open our hearts to him. God's love is defined as agape love, an unconditional love not based on merit. God's love is given to us not because of who we are or what we deserve. It is given to us because God, who is the embodiment of love, chooses to give it to his fallen creation in Christ. If you are one of the vast multitudes who feel that God couldn't possibly love you, or you feel God couldn't like me or love me as much as (fill in the blank), I want to challenge your thinking about that in this chapter, for I believe the scripture teaches us of a God who has a crazy love for those who are marginalized, who feel they are lesser thans, or just feel they are totally unworthy of his love.

In this chapter, we will explore a woman and her people group called the Samaritans who, though marginalized and hated by many of the fellow Jews, found a God, a Savior who loved them and embraced them as his own. This love they found in Jesus both shocked them and transformed many of them at the same time.

Their story is found in the gospel of John chapter 4, verses 4-42 which reads:

> Now He had to go through Samaria. So He came to a town in Samaria called Sychar near the plot of ground Jacob had given to his son Joseph. Jacob's well was there and Jesus, tired as He was from the journey, sat down by the well. It was about the sixth hour.
>
> When a Samaritan woman came to the well to draw water, Jesus said to her, "Will you give me a drink (His disciples had gone into the town to buy food)?" The Samaritan woman said to Him, "You are a Jew and I am a Samaritan woman.

How can you ask me for a drink (for Jews did not associate with Samaritans)?"

Jesus answered her, "If you knew the gift of God and Who it is that asks you for a drink, you would have asked Him and He would have given you living water."

"Sir," the woman said, "you have nothing to draw with and the well is deep. Where can you get this living water? Are you greater than our father Jacob who gave us the well and drank from it himself as did his sons and his flocks and herds?"

Jesus answered, "Everyone who drinks this water will be thirsty again, But whoever drinks the water I give him will never thirst. Indeed, the water I give will become in him a spring of water welling up to eternal life."

The woman said to Him, "Sir, give me this water so that I won't get thirsty and have to keep coming here to draw water." He told her, "Go, call your husband and come back."

"I have no husband," she replied. Jesus said to her, "You are right when you say you have no husband. The fact is, you have had five husbands. What you have just said is quite true."

"Sir," the woman said, "I can see that you are a prophet. Our fathers worshipped on this mountain, but you Jews claim that the place where we must worship is in Jerusalem." Jesus declared, "Believe me, woman, a time is coming when you will worship the Father, neither on this mountain nor in Jerusalem. You Samaritans worship what you do not know, for salvation is from the Jews. Yet a time is coming and has now come when the true worshippers will worship the Father in spirit and truth, for they are the kinds of worshippers the Father seeks. God is spirit and His worshippers must worship in Spirit and in truth."

The woman said, "I know that Messiah (called Christ) is coming. When He comes, He will explain everything to us." Then Jesus declared, "I who speak am He." Just then his disciples returned and were surprised to find him talking with a woman but no one asked "What do you want?" or "Why are you talking with her?"

Then, leaving her water jar, the woman went back to the town and said to the people, "Come, see a man who told me everything I ever did. Could this be the Christ?" They came out of the town and made their way toward Him. Meanwhile, His disciples urged Him, "Rabbi, eat something."

But He said to them, "I have food that you know nothing about." Then His disciples said to each other, "Could someone have brought Him food?" "My food," said Jesus, "is to do the will of Him Who sent me and to finish His work. Do not say 'four months more and then the harvest?' I tell you, open your eyes and look at the fields! They are ripe for harvest. Even now, the reaper draws his wages, even now he harvests the crop for eternal life, so that the sower and the reaper may be glad together. Thus, the saying 'One sows and the other reaps' is true. I have sent you to reap what you have not worked for. Others have done the hard work and you have reaped the benefits of their labor."

Many of the Samaritans from that town believed in Him because of the woman's testimony. "He told me everything I ever did." So when the Samaritans came to Him, they urged

Him to stay with them, and He stayed two days. And because of His words, many more became believers.

They said to the woman, "We no longer believe just because of what you said; now we have heard for ourselves, and we know this man really is the Savior of the world."

As we explore this story, there are some central truths we need to understand to fully understand the enormity of what this text is teaching us.

First of all, there was an enormous hatred between the Jews and the Samaritans. Think of it as a Hatfields-vs.-the-McCoys kind of hatred, a hatred-on-steroids kind of hatred. John 4:9 says, "For Jews do not associate with Samaritans." Jews hated the Samaritans, and the Samaritans hated the Jews and went to great lengths to avoid each other.

To give you an idea of how bad it was, most Jews would travel a whole day out of their way, crossing over the Jordan River and going around the Samaritan area located in central Israel to avoid any contact with the Samaritans and the area of Samaria (hey, that rhymes, lol). These two people groups (the Jews and Samaritans) wanted absolutely, positively nothing to do with each other whatsoever! They hated each other, were deeply prejudiced against each other with no desire whatsoever to reconcile with one another. Some things in our world never seem to change, for there is rampant hatred and prejudice today as there was then.

Why was there such an extreme hatred, prejudice between the Jews and the Samaritans?

What caused this hatred?

It goes back in time in Israel's history. Israel was once divided into the northern and southern kingdoms. The northern kingdom, at one time, fell to the Assyrians who the Jews deeply hated. As a result of this, many Jews were taken captive to Assyria, and many Assyrians moved into the Samarian area to police the land and put up settlements. In time, many of the Jews in Samaria intermarried with the Assyrians and created a mixed race called the Samaritans.

The pure-bred Jews hated this mixed, half-breed race of Samaritans because they felt, by intermarrying with the pagan Assyrians, they had betrayed their nation and people. The Samaritans were defiled, impure Jews, traitors to their nation and their God by intermingling their race with the Assyrian race. Along with that, they set up an alternate center of worship on Mount Gerizim instead of the pure-Jew center of worship in Jerusalem.

It is in this racially and emotionally-charged environment that Jesus decided to venture into the enemy territory (in the eyes of the pure Jews) of Samaria. Jesus knew all too well how these two races felt about each other but went willingly on a mission to the Samaritan people. Jesus is not prejudiced against any people groups but has come to be the Savior for all who will embrace him.

Jesus went into Samaritan territory and approached a Samaritan woman there at a well at about the sixth hour. The sixth hour would be noon, the hottest part of the day, the time of day when the out-casts came to the well to avoid the persecution of the crowds. The masses would come in the cooler parts of the day, at morning and night, to the well for water and the lesser thans during the odd hours. This woman was not only a Samaritan but also a grossly unpopular, despised one at that. That being so, notice how the Savior, full of love and grace, sought her out.

Jesus approached this despised Samaritan woman of ill repute and asked her, "Will you give me a drink?" She was shocked that a Jewish man would even talk to her at all. She points out the obvious. "I am a Samaritan, and you are a Jew. How is it that you are even talking to me no less asking me for a drink?" Jesus then took this conversation to a very stunning place. Jesus said to her, "If you knew the gift of God and who it is that asks you for a drink, you would have asked him, and he would have given you living water."

Jesus, the Messiah, the Savior of the world, was not only associating with this Samaritan woman of ill repute but inviting her into a saving, spirit-filled relationship with him. Jesus was intentionally seeking out this Samaritan woman and inviting her into a brand-new, born-again life in Him. Jesus was seeking her in hopes of saving her life and her soul.

In her mind, she was thinking of bodily, thirst-quenching water from a well which was a temporal quenching of thirst. Jesus, however, was offering back to her the soul-satisfying spirit of the Living God. Jesus contrasts the kind of water she was thinking of with the kind he was offering to her, the kind that eternally satisfies the eternal soul.

Jesus said to her in John 4:13–14, "Jesus answered, 'Everyone who drinks this water will be thirsty again, But whoever drinks the water I give him will never thirst. Indeed, the water I give him will become in him a spring of water welling up to eternal life.'"

Jesus knew she was a despised (by the Jewish people but not by him) Samaritan, an adulterous woman (John 4:18), a lost sinner, but none of those factors deterred him from her whatsoever. He did not pour out wrath upon her about her promiscuous lifestyle (John 4:17 and 18) but rather offered her a new life, a life of spiritual abundance instead of a dead, empty life that she was presently living. Jesus offered her abundance for emptiness, a born-again, spirit-filled soul for a dried-up empty, dead soul. The overwhelming love of God instead of the failing, faltering love she could not find in the arms of a man. This woman's history with men was the epitome of unlucky at love (John 4:17–18).

This Samaritan woman was not just spoken to by a Jewish man, much to her shock, but was being talked to by the Savior of the world who personally sought her out. Jesus goes on to tell her as much. John 4:25–26 says, "The woman said, 'I know that Messiah (called Christ) is coming. When He comes, He will explain everything to us.' Then Jesus declared, 'I who speaks to you am He.'"

Imagine the amazement of this woman.

Here's this woman:

- Going through just another day, going about her same old, boring daily routine
- An outcast Samaritan, an outcast adulteress
- A lost sinner without much, or any, hope
- A social outcast, a victim of extreme prejudice
- A woman looking for love in all the wrong places

- A woman looking for a better way but not sure what that way was/is
- A woman going through another rotten day in the midst of a rotten, empty life

Maybe some of you can relate!

Maybe this describes your life more than you wish to admit, at least in part!

Here she was, in the midst of another empty, mundane day and then God, the Messiah, Jesus Christ, shows up and everything—and I mean everything—is about to change, now and forever, for her.

And her response to the Lord's invitation to this new life in him? She said yes.

John 4:28–29 say, "Then, leaving her water jar, the woman went back to the town and said to the people, 'Come, see a man who told me everything I ever did. Could this be the Christ?'"

Notice she left her water jar behind (John 4:28). Why did she do this? This symbolizes that she had found the better water, the living water that Christ offered. As a result, she would no longer have to dip into the well of the world to try, in vain, to find what satisfies within, for she had met and embraced the one who fully satisfies within. She had met and embraced Jesus Christ, the true well of living water, the spring of living water, welling up to eternal life. As a result, she was changed, transformed from the inside out, born again in the Lord Jesus Christ.

In one day's time, with one encounter with the Living God, the whole trajectory of this woman's life was forever changed.

- The empty one within became the full one within.
- The seeker became the finder.
- The lost soul became the redeemed soul.
- The sin-scarred adulteress became the forgiven daughter of God Most High.
- The lost, despised outcast of earth became the chosen of heaven above.

- The greatly rejected became the wholeheartedly accepted.
- The unloved became the dearly beloved.

And what did she do next?

She went back to her Samaritan people and told them about the Lord Jesus Christ.

And their response to her testimony?

They came out of the town and made their way toward him (John 4:30). They said to themselves, "We are going to go check him out for ourselves and see if what she says is true."

And what happened next is doubly amazing.

John 4:39-42 says:

> Many of the Samaritans from that town believed in Him because of the woman's testimony, "He told me everything I ever did," So, when the Samaritans came to Him, they urged him to stay with them, and he stayed two days.
>
> And, because of His words, many more became believers.
>
> They said to the woman, "We no longer believe just because of what you said; now we have heard for ourselves, and we know this Man is the Savior of the world."

This Samaritan woman's saving encounter with Jesus did not just end with her but had a great ripple effect on the Samaritan people. She gave her heart to Jesus and was gloriously born again. She then shared her testimony of what the Lord had done for her, piquing the curiosity of her people—the Samaritans. They went to Jesus themselves, heard for themselves, and many came to a saving faith in Jesus. Revival broke out in Samaria, starting with an outcast adulteress and spreading far and wide from there. God did a miracle in her life, and God did a miracle among her people as well.

In one day's time, with one encounter with the Living God, not just one Samaritan but many Samaritans whose trajectory of life was forever changed.

Now I would like to take this Bible passage out of the Samaritan arena into our arena. What does this text tell us about God? What does this text have to say to us in this day and age?

I want to go back to the questions I posed at the beginning of this chapter which were:

1. Do you feel that God likes, or loves, others more than you?
2. Why do you think that?
3. If you said yes, what is your basis for believing as you do?

I am sure, if that question had been posed to this Samaritan woman, she would have said, "Yes, God loves others and God likes others far more than me." She probably would have said, "How could God love someone like me?" She probably would have said, "I'm probably the last person God would ever seek after and pursue. I am a Samaritan, and my Jewish nation hates us and probably their God, their Messiah, does as well. Besides how could God love me, a five-times-over adulteress?" I am sure she had a head full of thoughts like this continually.

But the truth is, she was dead wrong! Jesus loved her, sought her out, and offered her almost immediately his salvation, a brand-new, spirit-filled life. He was not scolding her for her past or present life but offering her a brand-new life, a brand-new direction, a bright new future. Jesus was not looking at what she used to be, what she was presently. Jesus was looking at what she could become under new ownership, under his Lordship within. And it didn't stop with just her.

It spread to her people as well. This marginalized people, the Samaritans, realized in a very personal way that Jesus came to be the Savior of the marginalized as well. If they would have listened to others, especially in Israel, they would have been told, "God doesn't want your kind." That would have been, in reality, the farthest thing from the truth. They found out from the Savior himself that they were sought out, they were loved and that God had a great plan and purpose for their lives.

Friends, not only was that true for the Samaritans, that is true for you. God likes you, God loves you, and God wants a relationship with you (if you don't presently know him). God loves you (yes, I said you) so much that he sent his Son, Jesus Christ, to die on the cross to save you from sin, death, hell, and from Satan's grip. He did that for you, for me, for the world, for the marginalized, the beautiful people, and everyone in between as well. If you are one of those who say, "I am not a religious person," he did that for you; and I challenge you to, at least, give him a try. You have nothing to lose and everything to gain. About this great love of God for humanity, the Bible says, in John 3:16, these words, "For God so loved the world that He gave His one and only Son, that whoever believes in Him shall not perish but have eternal life."

God so loved the world (the whole world, all the people, races, nations, the rich, the poor, the middle-class, all of humanity with no exceptions). He sent Jesus, his only begotten Son, to die a bloody, gory, sacrificial death on the cross to open wide the door of salvation for whoever would believe and receive him as Savior of their lives.

Jesus paid the great and ultimate price so that all who believe and receive him can be reconciled, redeemed, adopted into the family of God. About this, John 1:10–13 says:

> He was in the world and, though the world was made through Him, the world did not recognize Him. He came to that which was His own, but His own did not receive Him. Yet to all who received Him, to those who believed in His name, He gave the right to become children of God—Children born not of natural descent nor of human decision or a husband's will, but born of God.

Friends, there is a place in God's family for you, a place at the Father's table, a place in the Father's house, a place in the Lamb's Book of Life (the roll call of the redeemed), a place in the Father's eternal kingdom, bought and paid for by the soul-cleansing, sin-cleansing, life-transforming blood of Jesus Christ.

God has provided the way for all (no exceptions) to be saved, transformed from the inside out (born-again) but now, the ball is in your court. What are you going to do with it? God is a gentleman. He knocks at the door of our hearts, but the knob is on the inside, and it is our choice to open it. All we must do is believe in Jesus, his death on the cross and ask him to come into your heart by believing in him and receiving him, and he will surely come in. He will give you a brand-new life in him. When God comes to live in our hearts truly, we can never be the same ever again. Jesus invites all (John 1:12) to believe, receive, and be adopted into God's family. All means all.

As we close out this chapter, I want to ask you a personal question for you to answer in your own heart.

Are you trying to quench your internal thirst (the thirsty soul) with the well of this world?

Are you searching the things of this world, looking for the missing piece or missing peace within?

Are you looking for inner contentment, inner fulfilling, inner filling with the things this world offers? Honestly, friends, that is a futile search. The well of this world will always leave your soul thirsty again.

If we think a little more alcohol, drugs, sexual hookups, possessions, money, promotions, educational degrees, a prettier girlfriend/ spouse, a more handsome wealthy spouse, a finer car, a nicer house, a country-club lifestyle, or a million other things this world offers will bring the inner piece or peace within, it won't. Many people have those things, and many of them are still miserable and unfulfilled.

I urge you to try the well of Living Water, Jesus Christ, who satisfied the inner longings of the Samaritan woman, the Samaritan people, and multitudes of Christ followers, future and present. This well of Living Water satisfies the deep longings of our internal soul and wells up to eternal life as well.

This glorious Savior, Jesus, likes you. He loves you. He wants to come into your heart and saturate your soul with the life-giving power of his Holy Spirit.

John 4:13–14 says:

> Jesus answered, "Everyone who drinks this water will be thirsty again, but whoever drinks the water I give will never thirst. Indeed, the water I give him will become in him a spring of water welling up to eternal life."

CHAPTER

7

ARE YOUR BEST DAYS
BEHIND YOU?

And now the cry of the Israelites has
reached me, and I have seen the way the
Egyptians are oppressing them. So now,
go. I am sending you to Pharaoh to bring
my people the Israelites out of Egypt.
—Exodus 3:9–10

I have a question for you especially if you are an older, farther-up-the-road person and are reading these words. The question is simply this: Do you feel your best days are behind you? Are you feeling that your best opportunities are far in your rearview mirror, your glory days (if you ever have had any) are over and long gone?

If so, I have another question and that is: Why do you feel that way? Is it because your mind doesn't feel as sharp as it once was? Does your body not feel as spry as it used to? Could it be that some younger people have taken over and implied (or said aloud) that your services are no longer needed? Could it possibly be that you have just gotten to a point in life that you feel you have outlived your useful-ness—you are tired, and you are ready to coast from here on out?

Friends, if you are in that place, I want to challenge your think-ing on this and challenge you to consider the story of one of the greatest Bible characters of all—Moses. I feel one of the greatest lies from Satan is that you are too old to be greatly used by God and that far too many seasoned believers buy into that lie. I feel far too many younger people convey or imply to the older ones among us that they are to "step aside and let us take over."

God has a great plan for young and old, rich and poor, everyone who aligns their hearts with the heart of the Lord and desires to be used by the Lord to fulfill his purposes. God can use anyone power-fully who aspires to serve in his kingdom and perpetuate his glory. How do we know when our mission and work for him is through? I'll tell you when, and that is when you breathe your very last breath. Until then, God has you here for a reason.

As we consider all this, I wish to direct our thoughts to one of the great heroes of the Bible named Moses. Moses's biography has a powerful twofold message for all of us. The first message is that our God is a God of second chances. If you are one who has messed up and feel you have disqualified yourself to be greatly used by God, please read on. I wish to challenge your thinking on that. Secondly Moses's life has a great message for those who feel they are too old to be greatly used by God. If you feel that way, if you are convinced that is the case, I want to challenge your thinking on that, so please read on.

Moses's life, maybe more than any other in Scripture, teaches us that one encounter, in one day's time, with the Living God can totally, radically change the whole trajectory of your life for the rest of your life. One burning-bush encounter with God sent Moses's life, for the rest of his life, into the spiritual stratosphere for the glory of Almighty God. With that, let's dive in to the awesome biblical narra-tive on Moses, the amazing servant of God.

First of all, I want to look at the biblical truth that our God is the God of second chances. As we read the scriptural account of Moses, we see the younger Moses committing a sin that would haunt him for years. Moses, though one with the right intent, took matters into his own hands, getting ahead of God's perfect plan, and paid dearly for it. This sin, however, was a setback but not a terminal set-back. It ended up being a bad chapter in Moses's life, but it certainly didn't mean Moses's story was over. Friends, one bad chapter in your life doesn't mean your story is over either.

This difficult chapter in Moses's life began this way, found in Exodus 2:11–15:

> One day, after Moses had grown up, he went out to where his own people were and watched them at their hard labor. He saw an Egyptian beating a Hebrew, one of his own people. Glancing this way and that and seeing no one, he killed the Egyptian and hid him in the sand. The next day he went out and saw two Hebrews fighting. He asked the one in the wrong, "Why are you hitting your fellow Hebrew?"
>
> The man said, "Who made you ruler and judge over us? Are you thinking of killing me as you killed the Egyptian?" Then Moses was afraid and thought, "What I did must have become known."
>
> When Pharaoh heard of this, he tried to kill Moses but Moses fled from Pharaoh and went to Midian, where he sat down by a well.

Here we see Moses enraged by the cruel treatment of his fellow Hebrew, killing one of the Egyptian slave masters and hiding his dead body. Moses, though brought up in the household of the pharaoh, Egypt's ruler, had developed an ever-increasing sense of injustice about how the Egyptians were treating his fellow Hebrews and desired to rectify this injustice.

Moses was becoming increasingly aware of God's call on his life as the Hebrew deliverer which was a good thing. Where he got himself into trouble was by taking matters into his own hands instead of waiting on God's direction in dealing with this problem. There is a lesson for all of us here, and that is simply this: we can have good, godly, noble desires and aspirations, but we need to seek God's direction and counsel on how to move forward.

The right equation is: God-inspired burdens, aspirations + God's direction, leading = success and victory.

A recipe-for-disaster equation is: God-inspired burdens, aspirations + fleshly, carnal, self-led direction, leading = failure and regret.

Moses got himself in a mess by doing the latter, not the former. We can too if we are not careful. We need to seek God's action plan and not our own.

As a result of this mistake, Moses was being hunted down by the pharaoh. The pharaoh wanted to kill him, so he fled to Midian to escape the pharaoh's judgment. Moses fled, leaving behind all he knew and all his family and friends and was banished from Egypt.

Moses, now banished, met up with a priest of Midian named Reuel who had seven daughters. Moses eventually married one of Reuel's daughters named Zipporah and had a son with her named Gershom. Moses began a whole new life in Midian with his new family and became a shepherd. While Moses worked to make the best of this situation, starting completely over, there was still a great sense of unfulfilled destiny. Moses's heart still broke for the plight of the Hebrews back in Egyptian bondage.

Moses would spend the next forty years in the desert, day after day after day, watching over the sheep yet feeling like he was created for a far-higher calling than this. As he watched these sheep, I am sure there wasn't a day that went by where he didn't feel regret and a sense of "I blew it," "I missed my calling, my destiny," thoughts in his head saying, *You were made to be a deliverer, not a lowly shepherd."* Maybe some (many?) of you can relate to Moses's plight and frustration.

What Moses did not know at the time was that God was far from finished with Moses. God, who put the burden for the Hebrews deep within the heart of Moses, was preparing Moses through this season of his life, for his future work as Israel's deliverer. God had Moses in his "waiting room" and while he was, God was teaching and preparing Moses to be Israel's great deliverer in the process.

"How so?" you may ask. God had Moses learning all the ropes of the wilderness and desert terrain by shepherding sheep through it. Moses was learning every nook and cranny, every obstacle, every challenge the wilderness and desert could bring against the sheep.

God allowed Moses to go through this period as a shepherd, learning the ins and outs of the land and desert because he would later shepherd God's people, the Hebrews, through the same land. By the time his forty years of shepherding sheep was over, he would be fully prepared to guide the Hebrew people through this terrain better than anyone else.

Friends, God is not done with us. What God starts, God also finishes so don't give up and don't let up in your passionate pursuit of the Lord. If you are presently in God's waiting room, feeling bogged down, learn everything God is trying to teach you in this season of life. It may be just the thing that launches you forward to great works for the glory of God in the future. Everything Moses learned in God's waiting room was a major asset to him as he fulfilled God's future calling on his life. God's Word says to us of inevitable ebbs and flows of life, "And we know that in all things God works for the good of those who love Him, who have been called according to His purpose," Romans 8:28. God shapes us, molds us, refines us, and develops godly character within us through our life experiences, the good ones and the hard ones. May we get better through them, not bitter. The choice is ours. God knew exactly what he was doing in Moses's life. God knows exactly what he is doing in ours as well. We just need to trust him.

Moses spent forty years shepherding sheep in the desert, unaware that God was preparing him for greatness. All that time of sensing he had missed his calling, all his time of regret, and all the times of frustration about the plight of the Hebrew people who he so desperately wanted to help was all about to come to an end. Moses learned the lesson. Moses learned the landscape of Midian and the desert like the back of his hand. Moses's character was shaped and molded greatly by God, and Moses was about to graduate into a calling from God like no other.

We will pick up this story in Exodus 2:23–25 which reads like this:

> During that long period, the king of Egypt
> died. The Israelites groaned in their slavery and

cried out, and their cry for help because of their slavery went up to God.

God heard their groaning and He remembered His covenant with Abraham, with Isaac, and with Jacob. So God looked on the Israelites and was concerned about them.

Exodus 3:1–15 continues:

Now Moses was tending the flock of Jethro, his father-in-law, the priest of Midian, and he led the flock to the far side of the desert and came to Horeb, the mountain of God. There the angel of the Lord appeared to him in flames of fire from within a bush.

So Moses thought, "I will go over and see this strange sight—why the bush does not burn up."

When the Lord saw that he had gone over to look, God called to him from within the bush, "Moses! Moses!" And Moses said, "Here I am."

"Do not come any closer," God said, "Take off your sandals, for the place where you are standing is holy ground." Then He said, "I am the God of your father, the God of Abraham, the God of Isaac, and the God of Jacob." At this, Moses hid his face because he was afraid to look at God.

The Lord said, "I have indeed seen the misery of my people in Egypt. I have heard them crying out because of their slave drivers, and I am concerned about their suffering. So I have come down to rescue them from the hand of the Egyptians and to bring them up out of that land into a good and spacious land, a land flowing with milk and honey—the home of the Canaanites, Hittites, Amorites, Perizzites, Hivites, and Jebusites.

"And now the cry of the Israelites has reached me, and I have seen the way the Egyptians are oppressing them.

So now, go, I am sending you to Pharaoh to bring my people, the Israelites, out of Egypt."

But Moses said to God, "Who am I that I should go to Pharaoh and bring the Israelites out of Egypt?"

And God said, "I will be with you, and this will be a sign to you that it is I who has sent you. When you have brought the people out of Egypt, you will worship God on this mountain."

Moses said to God, "Suppose I go to the Israelites and say to them, 'The God of your fathers has sent me to you,' and they ask me 'What is His name?' Then what shall I tell them?"

God said to Moses, "I Am Who I Am. This is what you are to say to the Israelites. I Am has sent me to you."

God also said to Moses, "Say to the Israelites, 'The Lord, the God of your fathers, the God of Abraham, the God of Isaac, and the God of Jacob has sent me to you,' This is my name forever, the name by which I am to be remembered from generation to generation."

Here was Moses, as one who felt like he would die out in a foreign land as a discreet shepherd, as one who had felt he had squandered God's call upon his life. He probably felt like one called to greatness but doing a task he felt was useless; and every hot, miserable day out with the sheep made the sting of this much harder. He woke to what he thought would be another hot, miserable day of sheep-watching, and he could not have been more wrong. He led the sheep to Horeb, the mountain of God; and God Almighty showed up powerfully to him, and everything in his life was about to radically change forever.

God came to Moses, speaking out of a burning bush, calling him to be God's vessel to deliver God's people (the Hebrews) from the hands of Egyptian oppression. The deliverer (Moses) was prepared by forty years of learning the landscape of the desert, and the Hebrews were primed for their day of deliverance. God's time had come to bring their miraculous deliverance to pass. In one day's time, with one radical encounter with God, Moses's whole trajectory of life was about to change forever.

As we consider this, I think it's important to note some of the wording of this text. Notice what God says in Exodus 3:7–8:

> The Lord said, "I have indeed seen the misery of my people in Egypt. I have heard them crying out because of their slave drivers, and I am concerned about their suffering. *So I have come down to rescue them from the hands of the Egyptians."*

Notice the wording here. God says, "I (personally) have come down to rescue the Israelites." God said, "I have come down to deliver my people." God saw their suffering. God was concerned about their suffering, and God said, "I have come down to rescue them." God was going to rescue his afflicted people.

Now notice what God says to Moses in Exodus 3:10 which reads, "So now, go. *I am sending you to Pharaoh to bring the Israelites out of Egypt."*

God here tells Moses to go rescue the Israelites from the hands of the pharaoh and deliver them out of Egypt. So what is it? Is it God who was going to rescue the Israelites from Egypt (v. 8) or was it Moses (v. 10)? The answer is both! God was going to supply the miraculous power and divine presence, but he was going to do this work through his servant, Moses. Moses went out, with God's power, to deliver 1.2 million to 2 million Israelites (estimates vary). The point here is it is an astronomical number and a major undertaking for any leader. This calling would require large amounts of divine power and wisdom, both of which God would freely supply to Moses to pull off this monumental task God was calling him to do.

We would do well to remember what we read here for our own lives. God does not call the equipped. He equips those he calls. God does not call the powerful. He equips the called with his divine, all-sufficient power. God does the work (for his glory), but he does it through his chosen and called servants. If we are willing, God will see to it that we are able. That was true for Moses. It will be true for all God calls in our generation as well.

As we consider this calling/equipping aspect we read of here, I want to also point out the significance of one other thing worth noting in this Moses/God Almighty dialogue. Moses asked God his name so Moses better understood the God who he was talking to and to convey to the Israelite people who it was who sent him.

The conversation from Exodus 3:13–15 went like this:

> Moses said to God, "Suppose I go to the Israelites and say to them, 'The God of your fathers has sent me to you,' and they ask me, 'What is His name?' Then what shall I tell them?"
> God said to Moses, "I Am Who I Am. This is what you are to say to the Israelites. I Am has sent me to you."

God is referred to by numerous different names in scripture, each name reflecting various aspects of his divine character. I personally love this name the most. God here refers to himself as "I Am Who I Am," or "I Am." I think this is the most majestic and accurate way for God to describe himself.

"Why do I say this?"

"Or feel this way?"

By God referring to himself as I Am, he, first of all, is referring to himself as God forever, past, present, and future. He didn't say I was or I will be but I Am. He was God when he spoke to Moses then. He is I Am as he speaks to us now, and he is God I Am for all times. He is unchanging. He is God for all time (past, present, and future);

and he is totally trustworthy because he is unchanging, all-powerful, all-sufficient throughout every generation and forever. He is Alpha and Omega, God of all time, past and present.

God I Am is the all-sufficient God, and Moses needed to hear that desperately. Moses was called by God to a task infinitely larger than himself and needed the assurance of God's all sufficiency. By God proclaiming himself as I Am to Moses, God was telling Moses, assuring Moses, that he will be everything Moses and the Israelite people needed and so much more.

If they needed provision, God is the God of endless provision. If they needed strength, God had all the strength they needed. If they needed miracles (they soon would), God is the God of endless miracles. If they needed healing, God is the great physician. God is I Am. He is everything they (and we) could ever need. Moses's and Israel's inadequacies would be met with God's sufficiency. He was all they could ever need. He will be all we ever need as well as we walk in faith, trusting in the great I Am. I will say again for emphasis, Moses's, Israel's, and our own inadequacies are met with God I Am's all-sufficiency. Amen!

If we ever doubted the power and all-sufficiency of God Almighty, the great I Am, please consider this, God used Moses who was eighty years old when called and pulled off the humanly unfathomable. This unbelievable mission was accomplished, not because of Moses's power, wisdom, or abilities but as a result of God's all-sufficiency. Moses went out in faith and in the power of God to the most powerful nation on earth at the time (Egypt), brought down the most powerful man on earth at the time (pharaoh), and set the Hebrews free. By the power of I Am, the Hebrews were set free, and the cruel oppressive Egyptian nation was left in shambles. What was humanly impossible for Moses and Israel, God made possible by His all-sufficient power and grace. There is no other logical explanation for how something of this magnitude could ever happen except by the hand of Almighty God.

As we conclude this chapter, I want to share some applications from this text to our lives personally.

Application Number 1: God is a God of Second Chances.

Moses initially failed God, even murdered a man. Moses saw an injustice, took matters into his own hands, killed an Egyptian slave master and then fled for his life, as a fugitive, from the pharaoh.

Later on after Moses had learned from his failure, God came once again to him and fully restored Moses and used his life to accomplish a great task that we marvel at to this very day. This same God who did this in Moses's life can do this in ours as well. Our failures don't have to be fatalities. God is a God of second chances. If you have failed, return to the Lord, yield yourself into his merciful hands and stand amazed at what he can do in and through your life.

Application Number 2: God's power is not hindered by our age or weakness. His strength is made perfect in our weakness.

When others saw an octogenarian shepherd senior citizen, God saw a warrior prepared fully for greatness. If you are a senior saint, don't assume that your best days are behind for God may have a burning bush on your horizon. You may not be able to move as fast, think quite as sharply as in past days, or may not be as physically spry as in younger days, but Moses probably would have said the same. God, however, still chose to use him as his chosen vessel nonetheless. If you have a heart for God's kingdom and his work on earth, God, the great I Am, will see that you have everything you need to fulfill his call upon your life. God is not limited by how old or how young we are. God can work powerfully through all who align their hearts with his.

Friends, as we conclude this chapter, I want to challenge you to be on the lookout for your own burning bush. This same God of Moses is alive and well and looking for new warriors in his divine kingdom, those who he can work powerfully through in this generation.

Who knows? Maybe this very day, God may show up to you as he did to Moses and call you into a relationship with himself or a work of service in his kingdom that will be absolutely mind-boggling in magnitude and proportion. One encounter in one day's time with the great I Am launched Moses into a calling so high it was incomprehensible. By the power of the same God, Moses pulled off a rescue mission of humanity that is stunning in magnitude to this very day.

God, through his Son, Jesus Christ, is still doing works beyond belief through those who yield their lives over to his purposes.

Ephesians 3:20–21 says of this:

> Now to Him who is able to do immeasurably more than all we ask or imagine, according to His power that is at work within us, To Him be glory in the church and in Christ Jesus throughout all generations, forever and ever! Amen.

Our inadequacies are met with his sufficiency and in him, all things are possible.

CHAPTER

8

LIBERATION DAY

> For our light and momentary troubles are
> achieving for us an eternal glory that far out-
> weighs them all. So we fix our eyes not on what
> is seen but what is unseen. For what is seen
> is temporary, but what is unseen is eternal.
> —2 Corinthians 4:17–18

Many of you reading these words do not personally know me nor do I personally know all of you. That being said, I want to share a word that I feel accurately describes (your, my, and everyone) our shared human experience.

We all come from different walks of life, different earthly experiences, different professions, different family experiences, different socioeconomic situations, different educational levels, and many other varying life experiences. While this is true, I believe most, if not all of us, have come face to face more times than we have ever wanted with the following experience—which is frustration. We all have frustrations in life, heavy crosses to bear no matter who we are, and they come in many shapes, sizes, and forms. They can be very, very burdensome, and it seems at times that they are never going to come to an end.

For so many of us, frustration is there around every corner, isn't it? We have physical frustrations (we get sick, our bodies fall apart, we injure ourselves). We have financial frustrations (so many bills, more money going out than coming in, things breaking down at the worst possible time, so many things coming against us, exhausting our resources). In addition, we have relational frustrations (we get betrayed by someone we thought we could trust, we have family discord, for some, it's a divorce we didn't see coming and never wanted, a loss of a loved one that broke your heart). We have frustrations in our dreams and aspirations (our dreams/aspirations and our real-life results aren't adding up, we get so discouraged by all of life's obstacles that we stop dreaming altogether). And on and on it goes and where it stops, nobody knows, seemingly endless frustrations in so much of life.

There are so many difficulties, disappointments, and frustrations that we encounter through this journey of life. Being a Christian doesn't make us immune to the pain, hardships, and trials of living in a fallen, sin-sick world. That being said, being a Christ follower does make all the difference in the world in the midst of the fiery trials of life.

How so? First of all, we go through these difficulties with the abiding presence of Christ with us. Secondly we have the blessed hope of what awaits us beyond these earthly trials. That, my friends, makes all the difference in the world.

Today if you are in a dark place, a place of great trial, and can certainly relate to the fiery trials I mentioned earlier, I pray that the following words will encourage you and inspire hope in your heart. God's Word tells us, for all who are in Christ (and all who will embrace the salvation of Christ going forward) that there is most definitely a better day coming, guaranteed. While we encounter a lot of evil down here in this earthly realm, don't give up. Let's keep our hands in the nail-scarred hands of Jesus who suffered and then resurrected. Just like Jesus, we who believe will have to suffer temporarily as well, but there will be a day of resurrection for us too. As we remain true to the Lord, our story will end very, very well. Just don't give up, my friend. God has something amazing waiting for us beyond all of this.

With that, I wish to share three scriptural texts which speak to the temporal nature of suffering and the eternal glory in Christ for all those who persevere. These texts are Romans 8:18–25, and 2 Corinthians 4:16–18 and 5:1–5.

Romans 8:18–25 reads:

> I consider that our present sufferings are not worth comparing with the glory that will be revealed in us. The creation waits in eager expectation for the sons of God to be revealed.
>
> For the creation was subjected to frustration, not by its own choice, but by the will of the one who subjected it, in hope that the creation itself will be liberated from its bondage to decay and brought into the glorious freedom of the children of God.
>
> We know that the whole creation has been groaning as in pains of childbirth right up to the present time. Not only so, but we who have the first fruits of the Spirit, groan inwardly as we wait eagerly for our adoption as Sons, the redemption of our bodies.
>
> For, in this hope we were saved, but hope that is seen is no hope at all. Who hopes for what he already has? But, if we hope for what we do not have, we wait for it patiently.

2 Corinthians 4:16–18 and 5:1–5 reads:

> Therefore, we do not lose heart. Though outwardly we are wasting away, yet inwardly we are being renewed day by day. For light and momentary troubles are achieving for us an eternal glory that far outweighs them all. So we fix our eyes not on what is seen but on what is unseen. For what is seen is temporary, but what is unseen is eternal.

But we know that, if the earthly tent that we live in is destroyed, we have a building from God, an eternal house in heaven, not built by human hands.

Meanwhile, we groan longing to be clothed with our heavenly dwelling. Because, when we are clothed, we will not be found naked. For while we are in this tent, we groan and are burdened, because we do not wish to be unclothed but to be clothed with our heavenly dwelling, so that, what is mortal may be swallowed up by life. Now, it is God who has made us for this very purpose and has given us the Spirit as a deposit, guaranteeing what is to come.

Here we see the Apostle Paul (the writer of these two epistles) writing about how frustration and groaning within is the result of living in a fallen, sin-infected world. God created our world perfectly; but when sin entered this world, the world became fallen from its original perfect state, thus bringing pain, frustration, and groaning into our human experience. God's crowning creation (mankind), which was created in perfection and for glory, was plunged into frustration, groaning as sin entered the world, and creation fell.

The Apostle Paul says of this:

"Creation (our earth and humans) was subjected to frustration" (Romans 8:20).

"The whole creation has been groaning as in the pains of childbirth, right up to this present time" (can anyone say ouch?) (Romans 8:22).

"We, as God's people, groan inwardly as we wait eagerly for our adoption as Sons, the redemption of our bodies" (Romans 8:23).

"Meanwhile, we groan, longing to be clothed with our heavenly dwelling." 2 Corinthians 5:2.

"While we live in this tent (meaning our earthly bodies), we groan and are burdened" (2 Corinthians 5:4).

Can anyone reading these words relate to being frustrated with earthly groaning?

We don't have to be in this world very long to realize something is fundamentally flawed and not as it should be down here on earth. Frustration and groaning are natural and are the result of living in a fallen world.

You may be thinking that, for a book about hope and optimism, this section seems awfully dark and gloomy. That's true, but that's all about to change. Just as this section will change from darkness and gloom to victory and glory so will it be for all believers in Christ who endure the present dark hour. The Bible speaks of an end to this present frustration and groaning to a day of liberation for all who believe in and follow the Lord Jesus Christ.

Paul, who speaks much of the frustration and groaning, also speaks of God's rewards after we persevere through this time of trial, frustration, and groaning. Just like the Israelites were delivered from Egyptian bondage and given the Promised Land by God, so we will be liberated from our fallen nature and our fallen world as Christ comes to take us to our real home in heaven. We then will receive our eternal reward from the Lord. In one day's time, with the return of our Savior, Jesus Christ, everything will be eternally changed forever.

Paul says to us, inspired by the Holy Spirit of God, the following glory-filled words of hope:

"I consider that our present sufferings are not worth comparing with the glory that will be revealed in us" (Romans 8:18).

"That creation itself *will be liberated* from its bondage to decay and *brought into the glorious freedom of the children of God*" (Romans 8:21).

"We will be brought into our full adoption as Sons and Daughters of God, the redemption of our bodies" (Romans 8:23).

"For our light and momentary troubles are achieving for us an eternal glory that far out-weighs them all" (2 Corinthians 4:17).

"Now we know that, if the earthly tent (meaning our bodies) we live in is destroyed, we have a building from God (a glorified body), an eternal house in heaven, not built by hands" (2 Corinthians 5:1).

All these verses tell us that, in Christ, our days of frustration, our days of groaning are passing by and soon will be gone forever. Someday, in one day's time, by the hand of a merciful, gracious God of full redemption, our days of frustration, groaning, and pain will end forever; and our day of total, eternal liberation will come.

So what do we do in the meantime?

1. Be patient in the *sure* hope of our liberation. He who promised is faithful to deliver on all of his promises. He who promised will deliver on his promise on the day of his choosing.

Romans 8:24–25 reads, "For, in this hope (the hope of liberation) we were saved. But hope that is seen is no hope at all. Who hopes for what he already has? But, if we hope for what we do not have, we wait for it patiently."

God has given us a deposit, guaranteeing what is to come for all who believe.

Second Corinthians 5:5 says, "Now it is God who has made us for this very purpose and has given us the Spirit as a deposit, *guaranteeing what is to come.*"

God has given us his Spirit as a deposit, guaranteeing us of the glorious liberation to come. We will be delivered from this body of death, from this world of death and will be given a glorified body, a home in glory, and eternal salvation from sin, from death, and the grave. God, in Christ, has given us who believe and follow him the sure hope of eternal glory in heaven. We just need to keep on keepin' on in Jesus's name. It will be so worth it. One second in heaven will be worth everything we endured to get there, and all the rest of eternity will be bonus. Amen and amen!

As we await our day of liberation, we must also:

2. Keep the eyes (of our heart) fixed not on the temporal (the seen) but rather fixed on the eternal (that which is unseen, the eternal heavenly realm). Let us live by faith, not by sight.

Second Corinthians 4:17–18 reads:

> For our light and momentary troubles are achieving for us an eternal glory that far outweighs them all. So we fix our eyes not on what is seen but on what is unseen. For what is seen is temporary, but what is *unseen* is eternal.

Just like a racer racing toward the finish line, so we, as Christ followers, need to keep our eyes fixed on our Promised Land called heaven, pressing on with all the strength God gives us until we cross the finish line. Once we cross over the line, our pain, frustration, groaning, and discouragement will be forever gone.

Revelation 21:3–7 says of this:

> And I heard a loud voice from the throne saying, "Now the dwelling of God is with men,

and He will live with them. They will be His people, and God himself will be with them and be their God. He will wipe away every tear from their eyes. There will be no more death or mourning or crying or pain, for the old order of things has passed away."

He who was seated on the throne said, "I am making everything new!" Then He said, "Write this down, for these words are trustworthy and true."

He said to me, "It is done. I Am the Alpha and Omega, the Beginning and the End. To Him who is thirsty, I will give to drink without cost from the spring of the water of life. He who overcomes will inherit all this, and I will be his God and he will be my son."

God will, on that final day, wipe every tear away from our eyes. There will be no more death or mourning or crying or pain, for the old order of things has passed away, and God will make everything new once again. The one who overcomes (stays true and faithful, persevering until the end) will inherit all of this.

This is a blessed hope, and it is a sure hope because it is the promise of a Holy God who does not change, who does not fail those who place their faith in him and who is the essence of undefiled truth. God does not and cannot lie.

We need this assurance of eternal life because we human beings are creatures of hope. If we do not have a settled assurance of our eternal destiny, we cannot have settled peace in the present. We need to have the assurance about how our story ends before it does end. We need to know in our heart of hearts that our soul is saved, not leaving our eternal destination to chance. Our eternal soul is too valuable, and eternity is far too long to play spiritual Russian roulette with our eternal soul. A billion, trillion years is just the beginning of eternity. Eternity, my friends, is far, far too long to be wrong!

Jesus says that, in him, we can have the assurance of eternal life. In him, we can have peace in our eternal soul as we await his return.

From John 14:1–6 (NKJV) the words of Jesus says:

> "Let not your heart be troubled; you believe
> in God, believe also in Me. In my Father's house
> are many mansions; if it were not so, I would
> have told you. I go to prepare a place for you.
> And, if I go and prepare a place for you, I will
> come again and receive you to Myself; that where
> I am, there you may be also. And where I go you
> know and the way you know."
>
> Thomas said to Him, "Lord, we do not
> know where You are going, and how can we know
> the way?" Jesus said to him, "I am the way, the
> truth, and the life. No one comes to the Father
> except through me."

John echoes these words of Jesus about the assurance of eternal
life that is found in Jesus Christ.

First John 5:11–13 (NKJV) says:

> And this is the testimony: that God has
> given us eternal life, and this life is in His Son.
> He who has the Son has life; he who does not
> have the Son of God does not have life.
>
> These things I have written to you who
> believe in the Name of the Son of God, *that you
> may know that you have eternal life*, and that you
> may continue to believe in the Name of the Son
> of God.

Jesus tells us here that he is the Way, the Truth, and the Life
(John 14:6), the one who redeems us, who believes and brings us
back into salvation (right standing) with God. John the apostle tells
us that in Christ, we can know we have eternal life (1 John 5:12–13).
We can personally know Jesus as our Savior, and we can know that
we have eternal life. Soul salvation becomes a reality in our life the

minute we believe and receive Jesus into our hearts by faith. This is not a matter of chance, luck, being born into the right or wrong family but a matter of choice. God calls us into himself; and when we open the door of our hearts, he comes in, and we are saved. He who has the Son of God has life (1 John 5:12).

The minute we embrace Christ, we are saved, and Jesus, the Master Carpenter, begins to prepare a heavenly mansion with our personal name on it. Jesus tells in that same way, he will come to take us to our mansion in glory; that where he is, there we may be also. This assurance of knowing Jesus, knowing his salvation, knowing he is preparing a beautiful mansion beyond, in glory, for us gives us the assurance we need now so that our hearts do not have to be troubled (John 14:1).

Years ago, my parents and my wife, Cindy, and I went to the Upper Peninsula in Michigan (where we live) to fish for herring. One day, we went over to this hot spot for herring called Lime Island. To get to Lime Island, you must park in a public access lot and drive your boat across a five-mile span of water to get to the island. That day was a very beautiful summer day in Northern Michigan—at least it started out that way.

We went up to the boat launch, launched our boat, and set off across the bay to Lime Island. The trip across was very, very nice as we marveled at the crystal blue water and took in the majestic sights of the Upper Peninsula which is stunningly beautiful. After our five-mile trip across the bay, we anchored close to the island and threw our lines in to fish. We had one anchor in the front of the boat and one in the back.

About a half-hour later, I noticed that the boat, though anchored in front and back, was moving quickly in toward the island. In the short time we had been fishing, the winds had shifted directions oh-so subtly, and we were getting hit by whitecaps from off the bay. We quickly went from a very enjoyable day of fishing to a horrible predicament. The waves were pummeling our boat right into the heart of the big waves five miles from our vehicle and safety. It was a very scary, hair-raising, series of events and prayers started heading up to the Lord.

Shortly after we realized the severity of this situation, a great big boat drove up next to us, and it was the coast guard. They told my dad that he would have to drive the boat next to them across the bay with the pumps on to pump out the water we were taking on. In the back of the boat, Cindy, my mom, and I were brainstorming on what to do to keep the boat from being overwhelmed by the water we were taking into the boat. Our solution was a Walmart bag, a coffee cup, and a bowl. My dad drove the boat, escorted by the coast guard, and we bailed as fast as we could with the Walmart bag, the coffee cup, and the bowl. As fast as we bailed the water out, the more the boat took in as the waves crashed over the bow.

This was a very dangerous situation and the longest five-mile journey I have ever taken. What made all the difference in the world, though, was the presence of the coast-guard ship right beside us, guiding us safely across those violent, turbulent waters. We knew, because they were there, we were not going to perish, though the way across the bay was very dangerous, turbulent, and rough. We knew we would make it safely across because we knew our guide, our escort, was reliable and bigger than the obstacles we would face crossing over to safety.

The story parallels what it is like for all of us who embrace Christ as Savior and Lord of our lives. We still live in a very unpredictable world in which the winds can shift quickly, and danger can appear out of nowhere. This life can go from calm and serene to dangerous, hostile, and evil at a moment's notice. This world is that way for all of us, believer or unbeliever, saved or unsaved.

You may ask, "Well, if that's the case, what difference does it make to be a believer if we all are subject to the same problems, saved or unsaved?" That is a totally fair question. The difference is this: Jesus Christ is the coast guard in my story (which is a true story, by the way). We all live in a fallen, sinful world that can rock your world quickly and violently. The difference is this: For believers, we have a Good Shepherd (like the coast guard was to us) who is bigger, more powerful than the waves that crash in against all of us and who will guide us safely through the violent storms to the other shore—the shore of heaven itself. This Good Shepherd, Jesus, will safely lead his people, his church, through all this life throws against us, through the mystery that is death, and into the holy city beyond which is heaven. The journey across this span is dangerous, unpredictable, filled with frustration and groaning, but the final destination is glorious beyond words to describe, and it is forever. Friends, please don't miss out on this beautiful, glory-filled eternal home for the temporal fleeting pleasures of this world.

This same Jesus, the Good Shepherd, has come "to seek and to save that which is lost" (Luke 19:10), and he wants you as his own. He wants to save you, forgive you, give you eternal hope, eternal life, and to build a mansion just for you in heaven beyond. He wants to be your personal guide, leading you safely through this evil, unpredictable, lost, sin-sick world to a place of eternal love, eternal bliss, a safe haven for all who believe and receive him forever.

Do you know Jesus today? If not, this can be your day where the whole trajectory of your life can change forever. The stories of those who were changed in one day's time, all the Bible characters we have explored, can become your story and whosoever will believe in Christ as Savior as well. Their lives were totally changed with one encounter, in one day's time, with the Living Lord. This story can be your story. What do you say? You have nothing to lose and everything to gain. He has come to give all of us a brand-new life, the life God desires for us all.

Second Corinthians 5:17 (NKJV) says, "Therefore, if anyone is in Christ, he is a new creation; old things have passed away; behold, all things have become new."

This door to new life is swung wide open to us in Christ, but the knob is on the inside of your heart, and you must open it yourself and let him in. You will never be the same again as you do.

This same Jesus, who came at his first coming as Savior, will come again in the end, in one day's time, to bring to pass the ultimate day of liberation for all of his own.

God's Word says of this day in 1 Corinthians 15:51–57:

> Listen, I tell you a mystery: We will not all
> sleep, but we will all be changed—in a flash, in

the twinkling of an eye at the last trumpet. For the trumpet will sound, the dead will be raised imperishable, and we will be changed.

For the perishable must clothe itself with the imperishable, and the mortal with immortality. When the perishable has been clothed with the imperishable, and the mortal with immortality, then the saying that is written will come true: "Death has been swallowed up in victory.

Where, O Death, is your victory? Where, O Death, is your sting

The sting of death is sin, and the power of sin is the law." But thanks be to God! He gives us the victory through our Lord Jesus Christ.

Brothers and sisters in Christ, don't give up, don't lose heart, don't let the frustration, groaning, temporal trials of this life get the best of you, for they are oh-so temporary, soon they will be behind us forever and ever and ever. That day will usher in eternal blessings, eternal bliss, eternal glory, eternal relief, eternal joy, and eternal ecstasy that is incomprehensible in magnitude and in duration.

I am here to trumpet this truth:

Brothers and sisters in Christ,
Our day of full liberation is coming!
Our day of liberation is coming!
Hallelujah! Hallelujah! Hallelujah!

Our day of full liberation, in one day's time, in a moment, in the twinkling of an eye, and oh, what a day that will be! In that one day's time, everything will be changed forever. Amen!

"Behold, I am coming soon! My reward is with me, and I will give to everyone according to what he had done. I am the Alpha and the

Omega, the First and the Last, the Beginning and the End" (Revelation 22:12–13).

"The Spirit and the bride say, 'Come!' And let him who hears say, 'Come!' Whoever is thirsty, let him come; and whoever wishes let him take the free gift of the water of life" (Revelation 22:17).

EPILOGUE

As we conclude this journey together through this book, I just want to thank you for reading and hearing me out. I can't thank you enough. My prayer and steadfast belief is that the Lord will give each and everyone of you a one-day's-time encounter like we have read of in these pages. As a matter of fact, I pray for numerous one-day's-time encounters with the Lord for you during the course of your life. Be prayerful, be expectant, knowing that the God of the universe is looking to engage you in a life-changing, eternity-changing way.

I also pray that each of you will know that no matter how dark life may get in this world, whether in our individual lives or society at large, there is hope in the Lord. There is salvation in the Lord; and for all his redeemed children, evil, hardship, frustration, and groaning are temporal, but our glory will be eternal. Just hold on tight. Our day of liberation is coming—guaranteed.

I have often thought about what I would do if I ever won or received an enormous sum of money (hasn't happened yet, by the way). I have often thought about how I would try to bless my family, friends, and church, and how I would contribute from this abundance to causes I believe in. I would want to be generous, to share my blessings with others as I was blessed. I want to bless others as well. However, this has not happened (but I believe it can, in one day's time, lol).

That being said, I have received in Jesus the most priceless treasure a person can ever possess and that is eternal life and eternal sure hope. This is a priceless, eternal treasure, the mother of all treasures, and this is the gift I wholeheartedly aspire to give to all of your through this book. Jesus is eternal life. Jesus is the eternal priceless treasure—my greatest treasure. I pray that these words have pointed your heart toward him as your personal Lord and Savior. If you already know him, I pray those words have affirmed you and given you a greater sense of wonder of the majesty, beauty, and glory of Jesus.

I pray that God pours his matchless grace and his unfathomable, incomprehensible, and enduring love into the depths of your hearts and lives, both now and forever. God bless you, keep you, and cause his face to shine upon you, now and always.

Your friend and fellow servant in God's Kingdom.
Pastor Chris Slosser

ABOUT THE AUTHOR

Pastor Chris Slosser is lead pastor of Beaverton Church of God in Beaverton, Michigan. Pastor Chris is the husband of Cindy Slosser, his wife of twenty-eight years, and the proud parent of a sixteen-year-old son, Joshua Slosser. Pastor Chris has great passion for evangelism and inspirational preaching. Pastor Chris loves sharing the message of hope and salvation in Jesus Christ. He also serves the Church of God in Michigan on the state church health ministry team as well as serves in jail ministry and has served on short-term mission teams in Guatemala City, Guatemala, the last four years. Pastor Chris also does work in the Teen Challenge ministry as a chapel speaker, and his life aspiration is to spread the hope, the love, the salvation, and the glory of Jesus to as many people as he can as long as he ever can.

CPSIA information can be obtained
at www.ICGtesting.com
Printed in the USA
FFHW020614220619
53161425-58822FF